THE TEFLON RHINO

THE TEFLON RHINO

Navigating the Jungle of *Real* Life
(without Getting Stomped to Death)

Bill Wilson

NEW YORK, NEW YORK

Published by Metro Ministries
PO Box 409
Brooklyn, NY 11237
Web site: www.metroministries.org

TABLE OF CONTENTS

INTRODUCTION

Cautious, careful people, always casting about to preserve
their reputation and social standing, never can bring about
a reform. Those who are really in earnest must be willing to
be anything or nothing in the world's estimation, and publicly
and privately, in season and out, avow their sympathy with
despised and persecuted ideas and their advocates, and bear
the consequences.

—SUSAN B. ANTHONY

THE RHINOCEROS FAMILY IS distinguished by its huge body
and thick skin. A rhino can weigh as much as one ton and
has a thick protective skin that is about one-half inch thick
and extremely difficult to penetrate. The skin is a natural protection from sharp grasses and thorns. In general, rhinos do not live
in herds as other animals of the African plains. They are solitary
creatures.

Teflon is considered to be the most slippery substance that
exists. Its nonstick properties have revolutionized the world we live
in, right down to transforming the domestic art of cooking in our
kitchen. It has a high melting point, reduces friction for gears and
bearings, and is an insulator in electrical applications.

We live in a world that is desperate for the emergence of the teflon
rhino leader. This is a leader who has such a thick skin that nothing

can stick to him [her]. Too many of our leaders today are thin-skinned and unable to handle criticism and the inevitable pressures that just come with the job. In the face of their critics, they become frustrated, vindictive and overwhelmed. In the midst of pressure they must not implode. One who aspires to be a leader must be thick-skinned. They cannot worry about their reputation or their social status. They must know how to say "no" when everyone else is saying "yes." They cannot succumb to the pressure of the critic. To be thick-skinned does not mean that you have to be cold, negative, or difficult to approach. It does mean that you have learned to pave your own path rather than taking the easy way. It implies that you will not cave in to your detractors.

Theodore Roosevelt was right when he wrote these words.

> "It is not the critic who counts; not the man who points out how the strong man stumbles, or where the doer of deeds could have done them better. The credit belongs to the man who is actually in the arena, whose face is marred by dust and sweat and blood, who strives valiantly; who errs and comes short again and again; because there is no effort without error and shortcomings; but who does actually strive to do the deed; who knows the great enthusiasm, the great devotion, who spends himself in a worthy cause, who at the best knows in the end the triumph of high achievement and who at the worst, if he fails, at least he fails while daring greatly. So that his place shall never be with those cold and timid souls who know neither victory nor defeat."[1]

A teflon rhino leader does not live in the pack, but is often forced to live alone. The dynamic of their passion forces them to abandon the mainstream of mediocrity and begin the lonely chase of their dream. Their destiny often pulls them into a circle of commitment that eliminates all other fascinations outside that ring. When they are awakened from the slumber of indifference, they are launched into the solitary pursuit of what others call the impossible.

Those who have not seen the invisible realities of their dream worlds believe such people are mad. The contented are disturbed by their zeal and fervor. The elite misinterpret the driven actions of such people as a direct assault on them. All isolate them for fear of *catching* this horrible disease that challenges one to move outside the comfort of the traditional and conventional. They endeavor to segregate these people in order to safeguard their own comfortable and secure lifestyles. The teflon rhino continues on, in spite of the critics and detractors.

Being a leader is not for the faint of heart. The critics are always there waiting for you to fail and to remind you of your inconsistencies. The obstacles, at times, appear insurmountable. The pressures to conform, to compromise, and to give up are always there. However, the teflon rhino will not give in to the critic or to the conflict. Nothing can penetrate their skin. Nothing can stick to them. They are a *Teflon Rhino.*

Chapter 1

HOW FAR DO YOU WANT TO GO?

The road of life twists and turns and no two directions are ever the same. Yet our lessons come from the journey, not the destination.[2]

WHERE ARE YOU GOING? What is your purpose for being here? Those are questions that all of us are seeking to answer. It is important to understand your purpose, but it is more critical to know how to get there. It is good to know the end of the journey, but it is the journey itself that determines the end. The brilliant German writer of the 17th century, Johann Wolfgang von Goethe (1749-1832) said that knowledge is not enough; we must apply.

It is the journey of applying what we know that opens up new doors of practical understanding and the confrontation of what we do not know. I have met lots of guys who have their Master's degree in various fields of knowledge. Here is what I have discovered. Knowledge is no replacement for experience and common sense. Life is not discovered in a classroom. Academics are not a surrogate for what is learned on the road of life.

At the time of writing this book, I am working on my Doctorate. My motivation is not a great one, but it is a cool one. The only reason why I'm getting my Doctorate degree is so I can take it and put my degree in the face of all these smart people and say, "I have a doctoral degree, but I still drive the Sunday School bus and care for kids!"

> A seminary or a university might give you some tools for life, but they are no replacement for life on the road and the things that are apprehended on that journey.

I have discovered the priority of life. It is not the accumulation of knowledge. It is impacting and influencing people. That is why life can never be *experienced* in a seminary or a university. It might give you some tools for life, but they are no replacement for life on the road and the things that are apprehended on that journey.

I remember once that I was speaking at a conference, and afterward, this kid came up to me and said, "I want to get to where you are." He was all excited as he went on to say, "I've read all the books, and I just want to get to where you are." I looked at this kid, and I thought, *Kid, you really have no idea what you are asking for.*

Nobody wants to get shot. Nobody really wants to drive a Sunday School bus. I paused for a moment and then looking him straight in the eye, I responded, "Son, you really don't even know where you are right now, and if you knew where I was and what it took to get where I am, would you still want to go through what it takes?" The casual observer has no idea what it took to get where I am, and if they did, I am certain they would not choose that path. We want the glory, but do we want the cross? We must come to understand that the path to resurrection glory will take us by the way of the cross.

The Miracle in the Middle

Goals are important. Having a sense of what your destiny is will help guide your life. But here is the real truth. Knowing about your future is much different than *pressing in* to your future. This is the road less traveled. It is good to be a dreamer, but it is not enough. Dreams do not become a reality by some kind of magic. We are not swept away into our future by some pixie dust or magical elixir. Your dream must be coupled with passion—a passion that drives you into the lonely pursuit of what others fear to seek.

Success in life is about *going the distance.* The two hardest things in the race of life are starting and finishing. Life is more like a marathon, rather than a sprint. Sprinters don't have to worry about hitting the *wall. Bonking* is what marathoners talk about when they hit the wall in the middle of a long distance run. Your whole body wants to shut down. It wants to go on mutiny.

While your body is still running your mind is revolting and your motivation is diminished. Everything within you is screaming, "Quit. Shut it down. Give up." Only the distance runner knows that feeling. He also knows the joy of breaking the wall and going the distance. This is what I call *the miracle in the middle.* It is in the middle of the race where you confront your greatest crisis and where you also converge on your greatest joy.

How do you get there? How does one get from the basement to the penthouse? By way of the stairs! Stairs are roadways to your destination; they are not your destiny. The stairs have one purpose only and that's to get you from here to there. You don't live on the stairs. The stairs were not made to live on. You don't reside there. Now you can if you want, but that would be rather strange.

Because you bought this book I assume that you want to get somewhere. Your desire is to get to the place that God has designed for you. You want to fulfill your destiny. The desire is with you. The question is, "How do I get there?"

> If you want to go all the way, you must lean hard into the wind, push past the pain and not give up.

There are four roads that you must travel. Everyone starts their journey with a lot of enthusiasm. You are bursting with spiritual energy, feeling like nothing can hold you back. Somewhere along the way you will hit the wall and need to experience the miracle in the middle. If you want to go all the way, you must lean hard into the wind, push past the pain and not give up.

In order to complete the four roads you must ask yourself right now—*How far do I really want to go?*

The Emmaus Road—The Road of Recognition

And, behold, two of them went that same day to a village called Emmaus, which was from Jerusalem about threescore furlongs.

—LUKE 24:13

This is the starting point for everyone who wants to get from here to there—two men traveling from Jerusalem. The disciples are discouraged. They're disappointed. They're depressed. They're disillusioned. And why is that? They are on the road to Emmaus, leaving the city of Jerusalem. Only a few days ago they had watched their Master die an ugly death on a cross as a common criminal. All their hopes had been focused on Jesus. They were sure that He was the promised Messiah. He was to deliver them from the Romans and initiate the Kingdom of God on earth. They knew their position. They were going to reign with Him. These two men hooked their wagon to the Jesus show because they thought they knew who He was. They had such high expectations and they knew that they would have a special place at His side. But now it was all over. He had been tragically taken from them. They had been left alone.

They were so sure they knew where He was going. Unfortunately, they never got it. He had given them clues as to where He was headed but they did not grasp the significance of His words. Their own assumptions clouded their vision of the real future. They had left family and friends to be a part of Jesus' kingdom. The future was bright. Suddenly the brightness of their future was turned to deep darkness and their false assumptions had exposed them.

Now they are leaving Jerusalem. Behind them are their dreams and aspirations. Despair has replaced hope. Their vision of the future has been eclipsed by the disappointment and despondency slipping into their hearts. His horrible death at the hands of the Romans crushed all of their hopes and desires. Now they're walking down this road, leaving the place of promise. They're walking down this road, not knowing what to do or where to go.

I am sure that most of us have been in that place—the place of deep disappointment. There were times in your life when you were so sure of your destination. Your future was so bright and full of promise. Along the way people have disappointed you. God has apparently abandoned you. And now you do not know what to do, where to go. You have misinterpreted the signs of your future and now you are left alone in the dark.

Have you ever been so depressed that you didn't recognize your moment of opportunity?

Suddenly, out of nowhere, Jesus shows up and is walking alongside of them. They are walking down the Emmaus Road and out of nowhere, as usual, Jesus just shows up. Isn't that always interesting? At the least expected moment Jesus just shows up. And in their depression and discouragement, they don't even recognize Him. They thought that they had lost Him and when He appears, they cannot even recognize Him. Their melancholic misery blinds them to His presence.

Have you ever been so depressed that you didn't *recognize* your moment of opportunity? Your circumstances have so darkened your vision that you cannot perceive that He is there, walking with you. I remember the old time testimony meetings on Wednesday evenings when the old saints of God would talk about their experience and how they had walked with God for many years. The fact that they had walked with God was intended to convince them of the validity of their Christian experience.

We can think that we are walking with God without perceiving His presence with us. It is not enough to walk with God. We must be aware of His presence with us. We must recognize that He is there. It is not enough to be on the road. We must recognize that He is on the road with us. The disciples are on the road chatting with Jesus, telling Him all about their sorrow and disappointment, not even aware of the fact that the One with whom they are talking is right there with them.

Finally they arrive at the village that was their destination. Jesus has been listening to their constant chatter about the final events in Jerusalem. I suspect that there was a certain disappointment in Jesus. They did not *recognize* Him.

Jesus has felt that disappointment before. It was at the Last Supper that Jesus was talking to His disciples about His Father. Jesus tells them that if they have seen Him, then they have seen the Father. Phillip then asks Jesus to show them the Father. Jesus responds with a tinge of disappointment, "Have I been with you so long, and yet you have not known Me, Philip?" (John 14:9). *Have you not known me?* There is the problem. In spite of all that they had experienced in the presence of Jesus, they still did not recognize Him. They did not know Him. It was His great desire that they would really know Him, but they still did not get the message.

There was a time in my life about 22 years ago when I was dealing with a situation and in the midst of those circumstances, I went through an eruption of intense emotions. I never thought in my wildest imaginations that those kinds of emotions existed inside of me. None of us knows what we are capable of until our little world is rocked by unexpected events. What pushes your button? What trips your trigger? You overreact to episodes impinging upon your perfect little world. You are stunned at how you respond—shocked that those kinds of emotions exist deep within your soul.

I think that is why Mel Gibson's movie, *The Passion of the Christ,* struck such a chord with the American audience. I never thought that people would sit for two hours watching a movie with subtitles. But they did. I remember after one of my meetings, I was speaking with an elderly lady, an older Pentecostal woman. She began to tell me about the impact that movie had on her life. She looked at me and said, "I never knew that that's what He did for me." This woman has walked with God all of her life. It took a Hollywood movie, produced by a Catholic man to get a Pentecostal woman to figure out what Jesus went through for her.

I wonder how many folks think they know. Think they know why He came. Think they know Him. Then at a critical moment in their lives they don't recognize Him at all. Their responses to the situations shock them. They thought that they were stronger and more capable than how they reacted—stunned by their own lack of faith and their own weakness.

It was at a meal, a place of fellowship, that they finally recognize Him. You recognize who He is. This is the decisive moment in the story. They open their eyes and see Him and know Who He is. If you never do that, you are destined to end up in a place where your spiritual progress comes to an immediate halt. You cannot go any further. You must recognize Jesus in the darkness of your despair.

> If you don't recognize God in your moment of disorientation and dejection, you will not be able to continue your journey.

The Emmaus Road is the road of *recognition*—the road where your eyes are open and you see Jesus in the midst of your extreme disappointment. This is the moment of transition. This is your opportunity to make a critical course adjustment in your life. If you don't recognize God in your moment of disorientation and dejection, you will not be able to continue on your journey. Locked in your self pity, you will not see the doorway that is right before you.

William Throsby Bridges (1861-1915), was a Major General serving with Australian forces during World War 1—the first Australian general to be killed during the war at Gallipoli, on May 18, 1915. He wrote these poignant words: *Disenchantment, whether it is a minor disappointment or a major shock, is the signal that things are moving into transition in our lives.*[3] I have discovered that this truth has often worked in my life. Disappointment and tragedy are often the doorways to new places of opportunity, if we will recognize the God Who is there. Recognition of His presence is the first step of your journey, and it automatically places you on the second road of the trip.

The Damascus Road—The Road of Confrontation

As he journeyed he came near Damascus, and suddenly a
light shone around him from heaven.

— ACTS 9:3

The next road on our journey is the road that leads to Damascus. On that road we are introduced to a new character that will help us understand the complexity of our spiritual expedition. Paul was on his way to Damascus to do *God's* work, or so he thought. He was traveling to Damascus for the express purpose of capturing and imprisoning all of those involved in the Messianic cult that was creating such havoc in the Jewish community with all their talk about Jesus. They must be stopped. Riding on his donkey he is suddenly blinded by a flashing light from the heavenly realm.

The blazing light is so powerful that it knocks Paul off his donkey onto the ground. Lying in the middle of the road it is clear to Him Who knocked him on the ground. "Who are You, Lord?" He clearly *recognizes* that it is the Lord. This recognition will lead to a confrontation.

The second road, the Damascus Road, is the road of confrontation. It is sad to say, but many are lost on this road. At the point of confrontation they are ready to take a detour and find a more comfortable road. You will quickly learn that all other choices will lead you to dark alleys and dead ends. The road of confrontation cannot be avoided if you are going to reach your promised land.

You will have to make up your mind at this point. Will you shrink in cowardice and go back or will you find the courage to face what is before you? Before we move on to the heart of this lesson, we must understand this essential truth. It is not enough to get knocked on your can. It is not enough to be confronted with the error of your way. You must first recognize that it is the Lord that has knocked you down. It is not people. It is not the devil. It is God who is confronting you. He is confronting your place, and He is challenging your purpose. Paul is on the ground and he is now blind. He cannot see. Vision is lost but he recognizes that it is Jesus who is confronting him.

> When God meets us on the road we are traveling, our character is tested and success is determined by our response to the test.

Jesus is requiring change in Paul's life. It is not the strongest or the most intelligent who survive. It is those who are the most receptive to change. When God meets us on the road we are traveling, He is there to confront us, to challenge us. In that place of confrontation our traditions are questioned. Our concepts are examined. Our character is tested and success is determined by how we respond to the test. How far you proceed will be determined by your willingness to be confronted with the truth of God that stares you in the face. Life on the road is about change. We cannot enter into our destiny without the willingness to change. Those who are not willing to change are doomed to remain prisoners of their own fantasies and inconsistencies.

Saint Augustine (354-430), a Latin church father, is one of the most important figures in the development of Western Christianity. Augustine was a man of great wisdom and strength and yet a man of imperfection. He understood that life was about change and that change was essential to the journey. His words echo loudly to this generation. *"If you would attain to what you are not yet, you must always be displeased by what you are. For where you are pleased with yourself there you have remained. Keep adding, keep walking, keep advancing."*[4]

Only those who are discontent with who they are and where they are will be able to complete the journey. At some point you will be confronted by God. He will demand that you make adjustments in your life and in your thinking. Until you are willing to make those adjustments, my friend, you will go no further than where you are right now.

> We live in a world of contradictions and mystery. Our allegiance to God does not give us immunity to the harsh things that happen in our lives.

American Christian author Philip Yancey (1949-) asked the question in his book, *Where is God When it Hurts?* All of us have wondered why bad things happen to good people. It is not a mystery. We live in a world of contradictions and mystery. Our allegiance to God does not give us immunity to the harsh things that happen in our lives. On my journey I have discovered this dynamic principle. Betrayal, heartache, disappointment, and pain are often God's way of confronting what is in our heart and challenging what is on our mind.

To survive on the road of confrontation you must embrace God's grace and accept His confrontation. You must allow Him to change you, rearrange you. Your willingness to make those Divine adjustments will lead you to the next road of the journey.

The Jericho Road—The Road of Compassion

Then Jesus answered and said: "A certain man went down from Jerusalem to Jericho, and fell among thieves, who stripped him of his clothing, wounded him, and departed, leaving him half dead."

—LUKE 10:30

The Jericho Road—we are familiar with the ancient story but it is unfortunate that we don't really know the story. Familiarity with Bible stories often makes us immune and impervious to their truths. The story is a response to a question asked by a theologian. Who is my neighbor? In reaction to this question Jesus begins the story. A certain man has left the city of Jerusalem and is on his way to Jericho. While traveling on the road he is accosted by a band of thieves. He is abandoned on the side of the road, beaten and bleeding. The story picks up momentum as a certain group of people pass by the man left for dead. It is interesting that Jesus chooses religious folk to be the focus of the story. Have you ever noticed the contradictions in the Jesus stories? Usually the good guys are the bad guys and the bad guys are the good guys.

So these *good* guys, a priest and a Levite, pass by this dying man. They choose to ignore him and pass by on the other side. Here they come, a day late and a dollar short. They are on an important mission. They must get to the church on time. This guy is of a different color and they have no time for him. Their religious duty is more important than their human duty. This is the problem of religious institutions. They get in the way of doing what is right. Sometimes our religion gets in the way of compassion. We get so absorbed in our duties, but is it possible that our duties run into conflict with doing what is right?

When I went to Brooklyn, I thought everybody would be excited about what I was doing. I imagined them being so excited to support my efforts to reach out to the lost children of our city. I was 31 years old. With great excitement, I rented a Spanish Pentecostal church. The first building I rented to have Sunday School on Saturday was this Pentecostal church. I thought, *Man, this is gonna be great.* I was a bit naïve in those early days. It wasn't long before the pastor of the church confronted me and said, "The carpet is getting dirty!"

A couple of weeks later, he approached me again with these harsh words, "The kids broke the bathrooms." The bathrooms hadn't worked since we'd been there, but suddenly it's the kids who broke the bathrooms. It wasn't long before we were kicked out of that place.

Next we rented a Baptist church. This was a black Baptist church with folk from Jamaica. It was one of those "we four and no more" churches. They had no perspective of the opportunity that was staring them in the face—an opportunity to reach out to the kids of their community. This is a good thing, right? Evidently it was wrong.

We had over a thousand kids in that building. We were succeeding in our outreach to the community. The church had the old style pews. You remember the old style pews? Where there was no padding, just the hard wooden backs. The kids broke one of the ends off, and I tried to fix it. That's not my gift. I nailed it. I glued it. I laid hands on it, and it would not be healed.

The pastor invited me to preach the following Sunday. I was up there preaching when the back door opened and a very big-boned woman walked through the door. She walked in, and I froze. I watched her walk down the aisle, and I knew in my spirit where she was going to sit. She sat right down in the aisle with the broken pew. That piece kicked out and the whole thing collapsed.

> We have forgotten that the purpose of the church is to have compassion on the poor, the lost, the children and the forsaken.

We now have a pile of women in the center aisle. I'm looking at this pile of women and thinking, "We're out. We're out." And we were kicked out.

We have forgotten that the purpose of the church is to have compassion on the poor, the lost, the children and the forsaken.

Fortunately there are those like the Samaritan who get it. They understand that the heart of Christianity is compassion.

There was a girl that was a part of a church in Florida. While working for her church a burden began to grow in her. There was no audible voice. No burning bush. All she had was a growing burden for the people of Haiti. This was years and years before the massively destructive earthquake of 2009 that shoved that tiny, troubled and forgotten nation to a place of world media attention. What did she do? She quit her job at the church, sold her house, got rid of her car, and went to Haiti by herself.

Haiti isn't exactly a glamour spot for missionaries. Eventually, she ended up in the north on the Dominican-Haitian border. She lived in a classroom in a little Christian school. No electricity. No running water. One day while she sat in a restaurant on the Dominican side eating rice and beans, a little kid caught her eye. Those who have been in Third World countries always talk about the kids. It doesn't matter where you are, the kids are always there and they work their way into your heart.

> Your journey cannot finish until you have walked the Jericho Road, been challenged by the ones left to die in the ditch, and then give of yourself to care for them.

While this lady ate her lunch, this little boy stared at her through the window. The next time she looked up a guy with a whip stick that they use to beat cows had grabbed this little boy and was beating him. The kid was screaming. In a moment of compassion she ran outside and grabbed this guy. She started shaking him. The guy was shocked that this white girl confronted him with such force. He suddenly dropped the kid and walked off. She stood there on the side of the road with this little kid looking up into her eyes. She gathered this kid into her arms and began to feed him. That day on that road her entire life was about to change. She became a Good Samaritan.

Your journey cannot finish until you have walked the Jericho Road, been challenged by the ones left to die in the ditch, and then give of yourself to care for them. Some people get *stirred* by the need but are never *moved* by the need. They show sympathy for those who are hurting, but never seem to get involved in their lives. They will give money so that others can go, but they will never go.

Why do you think I continue to live where I live, in the same neighborhood in an old warehouse? I don't have to live there. I have chosen to live there. I can't get away from that place. I chose to live there. I don't want to escape the need that is always there, right in front of me. That's why I still drive the bus. When I get a little stressed out, that's why I go out on the road and I go in that underground basement apartment over on Troutman Street where six people are living in two rooms. Kind of puts things into perspective, doesn't it?

Let me share one last story about my heroine of Haiti. A few years ago horrific floods devastated Haiti. People were washed away in the flash floods that rushed like a freight train into the villages. In the aftermath of that calamity there were a bunch of kids who were left as orphans, living in an abandoned building. They hadn't eaten for days. Someone reached my friend and told her of the plight of these young children. They asked her if she could take care of them. They were dying, but what was she to do? She had no room to care for these destitute children. Someone had to do something and she became that someone. She got a bus and drove six or seven hours to get to that village. She loaded them in a bus and took them back to the orphanage.

Rolando, a little five year old boy, was one of those children. He hadn't been eating and had a severely bloated belly. They tried to feed him and take care of him. The first time he went to the bathroom, his rectum and six inches of his intestines came out. They were hanging out of his tiny body. This girl has no medical experience. She's not a nurse, but she took a wet cloth, pushed his insides back in and wrapped him up in a blanket. It was the middle of the night. There was no hospital nearby. The closest hospital is across the river in the Dominican Republic. But the border is closed at night and they will not open it for any reason until the next morning.

She picked up little Rolando and headed for the Massacre River. It's against the law to cross the river. There are soldiers all up and down the river with machine guns guarding the river. It didn't matter to our lady of Haiti. She would make sure that she got him the help he needed. Gathering the little boy into her arms she crossed the river and finally got him to a hospital. The little boy is alive today because of this precious saint—this Good Samaritan.

The Jericho Road is the road of compassion. It is the road where religion fails but compassionate people are born. How far are you willing to go? Are you willing to go as far as the Jericho Road? A good heart is better than all the heads in the world. Compassion trumps theology. True Christianity is not found in what you know but in what you do. Saint Thomas Aquinas (1225-1274) was a priest of the Roman Catholic Church in the Dominican Order from Italy. He was an influential theologian and a man who some consider to be the Church's greatest theologian and philosopher. He said that he would rather feel compassion than know the meaning of it.

You cannot complete your journey until you have been on the Jericho Road. It is at the place of compassion where your self-centered focus is adjusted and you get a new set of eyes that can see those around you lying in the ditch, desperate for your care and your concern. It is on the Jericho Road that you begin to think about others more than yourself. You leave the seat of the spectator and become a participant in the lives of others less fortunate.

If you are going to complete your journey, you cannot escape the Road of Compassion. The Jericho Road awaits you!

The Calvary Road—The Road of Obedience

Carrying his own cross, he went out to the place of the Skull (which in Aramaic is called Golgotha).

—JOHN 19:17

We are coming close to the end of the journey. The last road is the Calvary Road, the road of obedience. As Samuel declared to Saul, "Obedience is better than sacrifice" (1 Samuel 15:22). It is on this road that you understand that the pathway to all things in your future is the road of sacrifice. No great thing will ever be done without personal sacrifice. You will have to let go of some good things so that you can embrace the most important things of life.

> Technically Jesus didn't die on the cross. He died in the Garden of Gethsemane. He died to His will in the Garden.

I know what it takes to make a sacrifice, and I know when a sacrifice becomes a sacrifice. Technically Jesus didn't die on the cross. He died in the Garden of Gethsemane. He died to His will in the Garden. There in the Garden He wrestled with the will of His Father. Could there be any other way? When it was clear that this was the only way, then He submitted His will to the will of His Father. In that dark and lonely place His will came into alignment with the Father's will. His course was set.

His obedience was clear as He walked out of the garden and was dragged to the place of the cross. How far do you want to go? Do you want to go all the way? Then in the end you must walk the Calvary Road—the place where your will is merged with the will of God and only His will prevails in your life. At this moment you relinquish the control of your life. Your life is now in perfect harmony with His will and purpose.

It is at this point that you sacrifice what you are, in order to become what He wills. The road of obedience will bring you to your final destiny. There is no other way. You cannot bypass this road. There are no shortcuts. It is the place of death—death to your will. The decisions that you are forced to make will not be easy ones. But the reward is enormous. Saying *yes* to God will bring you to a place of resurrection. To gain what is worth having will require that we be willing to relinquish what we presently have. This is the way of the Calvary Road.

I like poetry, and I like to write poetry. There is a poem by American poet Robert Frost (1874-1963) that succinctly and appropriately finishes my thoughts on the journey and the roads we must travel. You might be familiar with it. It is called "The Road Not Taken," from his collection known as *Mountain Interval*. He wrote it in 1916.

> *Two roads diverged in a yellow wood,*
> *And sorry I could not travel both*
> *And be one traveler, long I stood*
> *And looked down one as far as I could*
> *To where it bent in the undergrowth;*
> *Then took the other, as just as fair,*
> *And having perhaps the better claim,*
> *Because it was grassy and wanted wear;*
> *Though as for that the passing there*
> *Had worn them really about the same.*

And both that morning equally lay
In leaves no step had trodden black.
Oh, I kept the first for another day!
Yet knowing how way leads on to way,
I doubted if I should ever come back.
I shall be telling this with a sigh
Somewhere ages and ages hence:
Two roads diverged in a wood, and I—
I took the one less traveled by,
And that has made all the difference.

All of us stand at a junction in life. All of us are confronted with two roads. The one road is heavily populated. It is the easy road, the road that most of humanity has chosen to take. The other road is the road of Christ. It is on that road that He calls us to take. Many do not recognize Him on this road and fear the confrontations and sacrifices that exist on this lonely road. They are prisoners of the religious system and never come into the compassionate way. In the end they do not take the road of obedience and their will continues to rule their hearts.

I call you today to consider the other road—the road less taken. It is a glorious, but difficult road. But on that road you will find your ultimate destiny.

There was a day when I chose that road and went to New York City. There were other places I could have chosen that would have been much easier. If I had taken the other road, I would not have to worry about finances and could have avoided the faces of the lonely children. I could have evaded the surmounting pressure that awakes me every morning. I wouldn't have to travel every week in order to raise the money to put gas in the buses and pay our staff. I wouldn't have to worry about the danger that surrounds me on the streets.

I made the decision to take the road less traveled. Which road will you take? That is your decision to make. No one can make it for you. One way or the other you will make that decision and your life will forever be affected by the decision you make.

It is my prayer that you will make the right decision and choose the road less traveled.

Chapter 2

WHERE IS THERE?

There is a land where there is no more sea—our faces are steadfastly set towards it; we are going to the place of which the Lord hath spoken.[5]

IN 1914 ERNEST SHACKLETON headed toward the Antarctica on his ship, "The Endurance," with the purpose of being the first man to cross the Antarctica. Sailing out of South Georgia toward Wendell Sea on the northwestern side of Antarctica, disaster confronted them. The expedition was halted when "The Endurance" became frozen in the ice floes.

They could not get free from ice, leaving Shackleton and his men trapped on their ship for over a year. When spring arrived they were still in the clutches of those frozen waters with no hope of continuing their journey. A thousand miles from the nearest civilization, they eventually had to ditch their ship and set up camp on an ice floe where they watched as their ship sunk into the frozen waters. With their camp set up on the ice floe they were hoping that it would drift toward Paulet Island.

After two months and failed attempts to reach the Island, they set out in their life boats and landed on Elephant Island. This was the first time that they had stood on ground in 497 days. It was clear that they were in serious trouble far away from any shipping lanes. Shackleton made plans to leave the ice floe with five of his men.

They took the best of their lifeboats with the hope that they might reach South Georgia.

Shackleton gave the order that each man was limited to two pounds of weight for their personal items. To illustrate just how serious he was, he discarded his own valuables in front of the men.

Then he held up a thick book and said, "This is the ship's Bible that was given to us by the Queen before this voyage. I am keeping only three pages." He placed the Bible down on the ice and held up those three torn, thin pages. Then he read one line: "Yea, though I walk through the valley of the shadow of death, I will fear no evil, for **Thou art with me**." In spite of their desperate situation, Shackleton knew that they were in a critical place but they were *there*, a place where God was with them.

For the next fifteen days they sailed through the waters of the southern ocean. Their lifeboat was pounded by the treacherous seas. Finally, they were in sight of the cliffs of Georgia. But this was not the end. They were trapped in hurricane-force winds and had to ride out the storm as their boat was pummeled by the pounding waves and powerful winds. The storm finally subsided and they were able, finally, to land on the unoccupied southern shore.

> It doesn't matter if you are facing danger or death, if He is there that place will be a place of safety.

After a period of rest and recuperation, rather than risk putting to sea again to reach the whaling stations on the northern coast, Shackleton decided to attempt a land crossing of the island. Leaving three of the men at the landing point on South Georgia, Shackleton traveled with the other two over mountainous terrain for 36 hours to reach the whaling station at Stromness. From that whaling station Shackleton sent a rescue to gather his men. All 28 men had survived the ordeal.

Where is *There*?

There is wherever Jesus is, even if it is in the icy and treacherous waters of the Antarctica. Shackleton understood the principle of the Presence. It was clear to him that if Jesus was there, he would be okay. It doesn't matter if you are facing danger or death, if He is there that place will be a place of safety.

Isn't it interesting how much has been written about a little stable in the city of Bethlehem? It was not a palace. It was a stable. This obscure stable became a holy place. What made it so special? It was special because of the person who was there. Jesus made the stable in Bethlehem a special place. It wasn't the stable or the city that was special. It was Jesus.

The Jordan River might be the most well known river in the world. What makes it so unique? The most famous baptism in the world happened there when John baptized Jesus. It was Jesus who made that river special. The Sea of Galilee might be the most recognized body of water, but I have been there, and believe me when I say there is nothing special about this place. The Sea of Galilee is just a big lake. What made it so famous? It was the person who walked on its waters.

What is the most famous nation in the world today? It is not the Babylonian Empire, not the Egyptian Empire, not even the Roman Empire or the Grecian Empire, not England, Russia, China, nor even the United States. What nation is the most famous and talked about today? You can't pick up the paper without reading about this nation. Where is it? Israel. This little bitty, tiny and insignificant nation is an extraordinary place. It is the center place of all of history. Why? Because Jesus was there.

What makes a land holy? It isn't the richness of its soil. It isn't the wonder of its terrain. It is because of the person who is associated with that land. It is Jesus. On whatever land Jesus steps, that land becomes holy and special. Where is *there*? The key to life is finding the *where* of His Presence.

I am not looking for popularity. I am not looking for riches. I am not in search of power. I am looking to find where Jesus is. If I find that place, I know that my life will have meaning. I am convinced that I will find peace, happiness, and joy. There is no other place in the world like the place where Jesus is.

Where is *there* for you?

What is *There?*

> *Get thee hence, and turn thee eastward, and hide thyself by the brook Cherith, that is before Jordan. And it shall be, that thou shalt drink of the brook; and I have commanded the ravens to feed thee there.*
>
> —1 Kings 17:3–4

When you find *there,* you find the place that will become a catalyst for conquest. Some people never find that place. Thinking that their way is the best way, they find themselves lost in a maze of dead ends and detours. If you don't find *there,* you will be destined to wander in confusion. I know people that have spent a lifetime trying to find *there.* In the life of Elijah we find some keys to finding our *there.*

The first key is when you discover what was there. God told Elijah to go there and when he got *there* the ravens would feed him. *There* is more than a place. It is not just a geographical location. *There* is not a platform on which you perform! *There* is not a ministry!

I was raised at a time when *there* was always a place. It was indicative of a place that you would go to and if you missed that place you were doomed. You couldn't retrace your steps and get back and make the decision all over again. This concept creates a lot of fear in people and immobilizes them. When you understand *there* is not just a place, it will make the will of God a lot easier to understand.

> Most people interpret this story incorrectly. They say that the ravens came to Elijah. The truth of the matter is that Elijah went to the place where the ravens were.

It is not only important to find where that place is. You must also understand what happens once you get to that place. First of all, it was a place of *provision*. Most people interpret this story incorrectly. They say that the ravens came to Elijah. The truth of the matter was that Elijah went to the place where the ravens were. And there's a huge difference in those two thoughts. Elijah was positioned in a place where there was provision. It was a place where supernatural guidance was combined with dramatic obedience.

I have worked with young people all my life. In working with them I have noticed that obedience is a tremendous challenge. They are so full of their own wisdom and think that they know it all. That reckless thinking has placed a lot of them in the wrong place. All of us have to come to the place where we begin to appreciate that we don't know it all. The key to life is in grasping the truth that spiritual guidance is coupled with spiritual provision.

Mary Geegh worked in India for 38 years and her book *God Guides* details the impact of her life on the people of India. Early in her life she was facing a major decision. She was in a quandary. What should she do? Should she return to America and accept the wedding proposal of Harry or remain in India? She sought counsel from one of her colleagues. Dr. Buchman told her, *"Mary, God will show you which to choose—Harry or India."* In the end Mary chose India. She became the headmistress of a girls school there and over the years, her life impacted the young people of that foreign land. It was in her book that she wrote these oft-quoted words: *Where God guides, God provides.* Her life proved that this dynamic principle is true.[6]

I have found it very strange that those who have never done anything in life have the audacity to advise those who have accomplished much in theirs. On what ground are they standing? Rather than be an advisor they should be the student. Whether you're 16 or whether you're 50, if you don't know what you're talking about, the rule should be: Don't say anything. Just listen. There is a Jewish proverb that states that there is no one as deaf as the person who will not listen.

Because Elijah listened to God, he found a place of provision. It is amazing where obedience will lead you. It is equally amazing where disobedience will take you. The road of obedience is always the *right* road. There is no other road for those who would seek to serve God.

How Do You Get to *There*?

I can hear you asking the question. How do you get to there? The first step to getting *there* is in knowing where you are right now. If you don't know where you are, you will never get anywhere. I have known so many people whose focus is way down the road. Projecting themselves into the future, they are trying to find the will of God. Here is the problem with that kind of futile and frantic pursuit. In the process of trying to find *there,* they miss *here,* and when you miss *here,* you're never going get to *there.*

Casting your eyes upon the future will blind you to your present and will prevent you from seizing the moment. There are open doors all around that many are missing because they are trying to figure out what could be, rather than what is. Paul understood the significance of the open door.

"For a great door and effectual is opened unto me, and there are many adversaries."
—1 Corinthians 16:9

There are doors around us, and there are things trying to prevent us from entering into them. But for those who are willing to see the door and enter in, they will find a life of fulfillment and destiny.

You Can't Get *There* Unless You're *Here*

Being *present* in the moment of opportunity is a critical issue of life. Most of us are present, but few of us are very present. I can tell when someone is *present.* I can see the glimmer in their eyes that tells me, "I am *here.*"

I remember the time I booked a trip to South Africa. The timing was right. The door was open. How did I know? A businessman from South Africa came and talked with me. I could tell that he was *here* and the passion was in his voice. "We are ready for side-walk Sunday school in South Africa," he declared. He continued to talk with such enthusiasm. "And I have come to you as an ambassador," the man said, "to tell you that the door is open for you and your ministry. As quickly as you can come, we are prepared to host you, and we are ready."

Every *there* is preceded by a *here.* Elijah learned that truth. He was available in the *here and now* of his life.

I could not get there until somebody knew they were *here.* The time was right because a door was open. I saw the open door and went through that door. Some people have such big dreams and aspirations of how they are going to live their lives. The problem is that even though they were *here*, they were not *here.* They were somewhere else. In other words, they were standing right here in front of me, but their thoughts were elsewhere.

Every *there* is preceded by a *here.* Elijah learned that truth. He was available in the *here and now* of his life. Your starting point is important to your ending point. You just don't get somewhere in a haphazard way. Things just don't happen. They are the congruence of a collection of decisions that you make in life where you are present to hear His voice and do His will.

Everybody thinks that taking a mission trip is the ultimate thing. *Let's get a bunch of kids and do a missionary trip to Mexico.* The kids go and do their little project. They take some photos…maybe even get a little diarrhea. Then they come home and tell their missionary story and think that somehow they are David Livingstone (1913-1873), the Scottish Congregationalist pioneer medical missionary and explorer in Central Africa. It was his meeting with Sir Henry Morton (H.M.) Stanley (1841-1904), Welsh journalist and explorer of Africa that gave rise to the popular quotation, "Dr. Livingstone, I presume?"

Going overseas is a great experience but a little trip does not put you on the frontlines. Here is the key: *you have to be here before you can be there.* There is some preparation that you need to go through before you can be successful when you get there. Alexander Graham Bell (1847-1922), credited with inventing the telephone, often said that preparation is the key to success.

Successful people are praying while others are playing. They are studying while others are dreaming. You have to be *here* before you can be *there*. American educator and poet Henry Wadsworth Longfellow (1807-1882) put it so appropriately with these words.

The heights by great men reached and kept
Were not attained by sudden flight,
But they, while their companions slept,
Were toiling upward in the night.[7]

You Get *Here* From *There*

You can only get to there from here because a *here* always precedes the *there*. Elijah was a Tishbite from Gilead. Now most people would look at that and say, "Okay. That was his hometown." No. It was way more significant than the place of his birth. When he was there—a young Tishbite, born and raised in a place called Gilead—he was at a place of historical significance. He was from the place founded by the tribe of Reuben, the tribe of Gad, and the half tribe of Manasseh. By Moses' permission they had settled on the eastern side of the Jordan River. The rest of Israel was established on the western side.

In the land of Gilead these three tribes built an altar. The other tribes were bothered by their actions. How could they build an altar on the wrong side of the river? They wanted to cross the river and annihilate their fellow Israelites. The three tribes explained to the rest of Israel that they would still come to their side of the river and make their sacrifices.

Who is willing to build an altar—a place of sacrifice where God's Word is more important than our word?

The rest of Israel did not get it. They were still puzzled. Why did they still feel like they needed an altar on their side? The tribes made this very compelling argument. "What would happen to us over on this side of the river if you guys over there where the altar is, would suddenly turn your backs on the one, true God? We're building our own altar just in case you turn your backs on Jehovah."

There is a lot of building happening in the body of Christ today. Buildings are being constructed. Ministries are being established. But here is the question I have. Is anyone building an altar? In the midst of all this construction, who is willing to build an altar—a place of sacrifice where God's Word is more important than our word? You had better build that altar. Someday you are going to need it. Too many ministries have lost their way because they never built an altar.

A while back I returned to the place where I had attended church on 16th Street in St. Petersburg, Florida. There was no building. Only an empty lot! How could this be? What happened? Standing there my thoughts went back to the guy who was the youth pastor at that church. He had taught me how to put Gospel tracts in a phone booth. I was too afraid to hand them out on the street. Out of curiosity, I tried to track this guy down. I found out that he was in prison for attempted murder. What happened? How could my mentor be in prison? When I look back on my past, most of those folk are gone. They are all gone. They never built an altar.

Here I am after all these years. Why? It doesn't matter to me what others do. Years ago I learned that I had better build my own altar right here, right now. I couldn't trust what others have done or would do. I had to make my own place of sacrifice just in case. People will come and go out of your life. What counts is what you have done to prepare yourself.

Elijah grew up in this historical place—this sacred place made holy by the acts of those who had gone before him. Elijah contemplated their actions and then he acted. He remembered the story of Gideon from the tribe of Manasseh. God had chosen him to defeat those that were worshipping Baal. Remember the story? God whittled down his army from 20,000 to 300. God does have some unusual strategies at times.

This much I know. God's ways are always better than our ways. I would rather have 300 prepared and committed folk than 20,000 uncertain and unprepared folk. Those 300 were the right people with the right motivation. It was a lesson that Elijah would never forget.

I grew up in a time and a place where there were real missionaries. They just didn't take little jaunts into the Third World. They didn't go to visit. They went to stay. They lived their lives in poverty and with sickness. They sacrificed their lives for the people around them. They weren't looking for large crowds. They were looking for the poor and disenfranchised of this world. You won't know these people. They haven't written books. No one knows them. But I knew them, and God knew them. They are my heroes. Charles Greenaway. Mark Buntain. Morris Plutz.

People today are more interested in what they can get out of the ministry as opposed to what they can give. They are more interested in titles as opposed to anonymity. When I came to New York City I had only one thought, *If those guys could do it, let's give it a shot.* Their altar became my altar. There is a world out there that somebody needs to reach and it might as well be me who reaches it. I am not waiting for others who have their eyes glazed over with visions of grandeur. I am too busy putting my hand to the plow. In my own way, I am trying to preserve the spirit of those who have gone before me. I am trying to let my life reflect the sacrifices they have made.

Elijah the Tishbite grew up watching the men and women of God step out in faith. They were not perfect, but they were brave men and women who were willing to count the cost and get into the battle. They were men and women of faith. They built their own altar and when Elijah came on the scene, he made a decision to follow in their steps.

Now it is my time. It is my prayer that there will be young people who will look at my life and say that they will follow Christ as I have followed Christ. I pray that the altar that I have built will be a testimony for others to build their own altar.

Where is *There*?

It was round about eighteen thousand measures: and the name of the city from that day shall be, The LORD is there.
—EZEKIEL 48:35

Ezekiel is one of the great prophetic books of the Bible. It was written about 1600 BC by a prophet of God who had preached with all of his heart for over 22 years while exiled in Babylon. He had lost his wife. He had lost his nation. He watched as the Babylonians destroyed Jerusalem and then he was hauled away in chains to Babylon. He was now all alone. In chapter 48 he was reaching the end of his message. I am sure that Ezekiel wondered what would happen next. When all the labor and sacrifice and hardships are finished, where will we be?

Ezekiel stepped into the prophetic zone as he had done so many times before. Before his eyes he saw the people of God and described the place that awaited them. After the description of the city of God he ended it with these dynamic words that echo through the halls of time to us today. *The name of that great city is: The Lord is there. The Lord is there. The Lord is there* (see Ezekiel 48:35).

Wherever God is—that is a good place, a perfect place. That is the place that waits for you and for me.

After it's all done, friend, we have a promise that we will be somewhere where He will always be. We will be with Him forever. Too many people are curious as to what will be there. I just want to know that He will be there. Wherever God is—that is a good place, a perfect place. That is the place that waits for you and for me. The name of that great city will be, "The Lord is there." And where He is, we shall be also. It will be our last *there*. It is the place of our final destination.

Every sacrifice of our life strikes a chord that will vibrate in eternity. Eternity awaits us. He awaits us, and when we get to *there*, all of our *here* will be worth it. Your *there* will always be preceded by your *here*. Work while it is still day for the night is coming when no man can work (see John 9:4), and we will finally be there. Decide today that you will be *here*, so that one day you will be *there*—in that city that is called *The Lord is there.*

Chapter 3

IF YOU CAN'T SEE IT, IT'S NOT REAL

Faith isn't the ability to believe long and far into the misty future. It's simply taking God at His Word and taking the next step.[8]

THERE ARE MOMENTS IN every life where something happens that turns out to be a defining moment. We cannot predict or even imagine how or when that time will encroach upon the normality of our daily existence. Joni Eareckson Tada had one of those moments in 1967 when a diving accident left her hospitalized and paralyzed. Lying on a hospital bed at a point of deep despair she went so far as to ask her friends to help her commit suicide. She did not want to face life without the possibility of ever walking again.

Fortunately, she had good friends who ignored that frantic request. It took her two years of intense rehabilitation before she was finally able to leave the hospital. With renewed purpose and determination, Joni abandoned a potential life of self-pity and gave herself to the service of others. Because of the many friends who stood with her in those days, she formed her own ministry called *Joni and Friends*.

I had my own defining moment a few years ago on the streets of New York. I have written about this story before, but it is important to tell it again. It was the closest call to death I have ever had. I was accosted by a robber on the street. I have been in some tough places before, and I was certain I could get out of this one. I knew I was in trouble when the guy put a gun in my face and pulled the trigger. The first attempt misfired. The second shot went off and blew a hole in the side of my face. The guy ran away, and somehow I got to my car and drove myself to the hospital. I thought I could get to the hospital faster than waiting for an ambulance to come and get me.

After recovering, I spent time reflecting on all that had transpired. Often we are not able to appreciate the significance of a moment until it has passed. While you are in the moment, you are simply trying to survive. All of us have had those moments when we feel like we cannot survive—we cannot possibly live another day. You just want to shut the door to your room, climb into bed, put the pillow over your head, and wait for everything to pass.

After the time has passed, you look back and say, "Wow! I made it. God was working in my life through all of the circumstances. I found His grace to get through those times." I was surprised that there were friends there who supported me. I learned some things that I could not have learned any other way.

In Mark chapter two, a man sick with palsy had a defining moment.

The Word Draws the Crowd

And again he entered into Capernaum after some days; and it was noised that he was in the house. And straightway many were gathered together, insomuch that there was no room to receive them, no, not so much as about the door: and he preached the word unto them.

And they come unto him, bringing one sick of the palsy, which was borne of four. And when they could not come nigh unto him for the press, they uncovered the roof where he was: and when they had broken it up, they let down the bed wherein the sick of the palsy lay. When Jesus saw their faith, he said unto the sick of the palsy, Son, thy sins be forgiven thee.

—MARK 2:1-5

In today's Christian community our language is filled with clichés and buzzwords. Empty clichés that are grown in the greenhouse of empty religion have always been a problem for the Church. A *cliché* is defined by Webster as "a trite phrase or expression; a platitude, a tired phrase, hackneyed, stereotyped." Get the picture? A cliché is something that *has lost originality, ingenuity, and impact by <u>long overuse</u>.*[9]

One of the great overused and misused words of our time is the word *faith*. The problem with buzzwords is that they carry different meaning depending on the person who is using them. The word *faith* has been annihilated by television evangelists using this word to support their own cause.

So when most people talk about faith, it is used in abstract terms that have no depth of meaning. For some people faith becomes magical. If you have faith, you will get a new car, money in the bank, and your house will be paid for.

I believe in the importance of faith. Without faith my life would be insignificant. But it is not the same kind of faith that I hear talked about in many churches across this country. Faith needs to be redefined for this generation. The faith that I believe in is the faith that *Jesus saw* in the lives of the four friends of this man with the palsy. It wasn't blind faith. It was visible faith, as we will see.

 Jesus didn't need any advertisement to get people to come and hear Him speak.

The story begins with Jesus going by himself to a house in Capernaum. The story does not tell us whose house it was. Jesus shows up with no fanfare, no advertisement, no flyers, no newspaper announcements, and no PR campaign. What did He do when He got to the house? He preached the Word to them.

He preached the *logos* (the Word) to them. It was not a healing meeting. Jesus was preaching salvation to those who were in the house. Jesus didn't need any advertisement to get people to come and hear Him speak. As soon as people found out that Jesus was in town, they flocked to Him. The people flocked to hear Jesus at this little, flat-roofed house in Capernaum. People were actually now outside surrounding the house trying to hear, trying to get to Jesus. The place was packed. You just know something wonderful is going to happen. It always does when Jesus shows up.

Somebody to Lean On

In another part of the city there is a man with the palsy. *Palsy* is "a paralysis of the body that is usually accompanied by uncontrolled movement of a body part," according to the dictionary. We don't know where the paralysis had attacked his body. We just know that he could not walk.

The thing that caught my attention about this story is that it does not play out like most of the New Testament miracles: blind Bartimaeus (see Mark 10:46), the woman with the issue of blood (see Luke 8:43-48), the man with the withered hand (see Luke 3:1-6), all of these had a point of reference and saw Jesus as the answer to their need. Something happened that drew them to reach out to Jesus. They had either heard about Jesus or had seen Him perform miracles. So when they pressed toward Him, there was a reason why they were doing it. There was a point of reference.

But with this paralytic, there was no point of reference. He had evidently heard nothing and had seen nothing concerning this man Jesus. He was dependent upon others who had heard about Jesus. This man who was the cripple did not have a point of reference that would give him any hope to lean on, but his friends did.

All of us have been at this point. We are paralyzed by a situation. We have lost a job. We have found out that we have cancer. People have betrayed us. We are alone and desperate for someone to help us. We need somebody to lean on. It's like the old Bill Withers song:

> *Lean on me, when you're not strong*
> *And I'll be your friend*
> *I'll help you carry on*
> *For it won't be long*
> *'Til I'm gonna need*
> *Somebody to lean on*[10]

Everybody needs somebody to lean on. We were not created to walk alone. After Cain had murdered his brother Abel, the Lord confronted Cain and asked him, "Where is your brother?" In response Cain retorted, "Am I my brother's keeper?" (Genesis 4:9). Well, it is clear that God created us to be our brother's keeper. We are responsible for those around us. We cannot turn a blind eye to those in need. The principle key of the body of Christ is that we were meant to live our lives in service to one another. We are responsible to those around us. We were never meant to turn the blind eye.

Fortunately for this guy, he had four friends to lean on. He didn't have to ask them. They were there in his time of need. They just said, "This guy is sick. Something's wrong with him." And, collectively, they were concerned enough about him that they said, "We had better take him to Jesus." They had heard the wonderful stories of Jesus and they knew that if they could just get their friend to Jesus, he would be healed. Finding the house was not the issue. Location is not the issue. *Who* is there is the critical point. Finding Jesus was the issue!

It's not enough to just bring somebody to church. You have to find a way to get them to Jesus.

It's not about bringing somebody to the house. It's not enough to just bring somebody to church. *Let's just get them to the church.* That is not enough. You have to find a way to get them to Jesus. This is the heart and the way of a true soul winner and a true friend. Get them to Jesus!

What will you do when you are faced with human need? How will you react? Will you just ignore them and go on your way? Remember the Jericho Road? Will you be like the religious folk or like the Good Samaritan?

The four guys saw their friend was in great need. They realized the urgency of the moment. They had heard that Jesus was in town and they knew they needed to get their friend to Him. They understood that we are our brothers' keepers. The great Warsaw-born American Jewish rabbi, philosopher and civil rights activist Abraham Joshua Heschel (1907-1972) understood that all of us are responsible to show compassion to those who are hurting, rejected, and ostracized. Heschel described this human responsibility in this way: *A religious man is a person who holds God and man in one thought at one time, at all times, who suffers harm done to others, whose greatest passion is compassion, whose greatest strength is love and defiance of despair.*[11]

Unfortunately there are few who understand that if one goes down, we all go down. That is the dynamic principle of the body of

Christ. If we know that it is within our power to help someone, and we choose to lock up our bowels of compassion, I believe we will be held accountable for it. The musketeer motto is true: *One for all, and all for one!*

The Miracle of Friends

There are times for all of us when our faith wavers. Paralyzed by our circumstances we can become frozen in our own apathy and doubt. It is at this point in our lives when friends are important. We were never meant to live our lives in a vacuum—isolated from the strength and encouragement that others can supply. We need the faith of the four. Those who isolate themselves from others are fools. You'd better surround yourself with people who do have faith.

This miracle was not moved into motion because of that man's faith. It was put into motion because of someone else's faith for him. Isn't that good? I guess that's a pretty good argument for the truth that you had better be careful who your friends are. It is critical that the friends who surround you are people of faith and people who are committed to you.

The older I get, the more wary I am of the people that I spend time with. I want to be around people who have faith. I need to have friends. I need to be surrounded by people of great faith. Why? Because someday may come when it is possible that my faith isn't what it needs to be. I admit that there are times when I get discouraged. There are times when I need the miracle of a good friend. Give me some friends who know God and are protecting my back.

The cripple's friends looked at him in his despondency and despair and said, "We can't just leave him here to die." They had a choice. They could have decided that they didn't have time to help this man. The thoughts could have crossed their minds: *Hey, we each have our own problems. We don't have time to get this man to*

Jesus. They were moved by compassion for their friend. They realized that if they didn't do something, he was going to die. They were challenged by the emergency of the moment and acted!

> Somebody somewhere has to look out at a generation and say, "If we don't do something, who will?"

We stand on the precipice of urgent times. If we don't do something, there's a whole generation of folks who are going to die. Somebody somewhere has to look out at a generation and say, "If we don't do something, who will? Who? Who in this city is going to do it?" Our cities are in the throes of death—death by poverty, death by crime, and death by drugs. Where are the people who care? Where are the ones who will act?

We still have preachers up in Harlem selling personal prophecies for two hundred and fifty dollars apiece. I have watched every shyster come into this city and do his thing. They are seeking to get rich on the backs of the poor. Where are the friends who care for others? Where are those men and women of faith who will sacrifice their lives for the good of others? Too many have abandoned the storefront and the poor to build their fancy buildings and minister to the rich.

People still ask me, "How come you still go to small churches and preach?" I'll always go to small churches, because when I first got involved in ministry, the only people who would have me were the small churches. I don't despise the big churches. I don't avoid television. These places give me great opportunities to raise the money we need to sustain this work in New York. But I will never forget that it was those small churches in the beginning that supported me.

I believe in the Jesus way. He came to seek and save those who are lost. He had his eyes on the disabled and disenfranchised. I have a lot of respect for Mother Teresa (1910-1997), an Albanian Catholic nun with Indian citizenship. For over 45 years she ministered to the poor, sick, orphaned, and dying, while guiding the Missionaries of Charity's expansion, first throughout India and then in other countries. These are the powerful words that guided her life. *"Let us touch the dying, the poor, the lonely and the unwanted according to the graces we have received and let us not be ashamed or slow to do the humble work."*[12]

Doors of Opportunity

Every one of us has a key that will help someone else. These four friends did not miss the opportunity that was staring them in the face. Here was a guy that had a need. They knew Someone who could fix him right up. It was an opportunity to do something good.

All of us have been confronted with great opportunities that are often masked by a precarious predicament. Sometimes we can't see the door because it is camouflaged by difficulty. The courageous only have eyes for the door. That was all that these four friends saw. They were not blinded by their friend's impossible situation. They didn't see the problem. All they saw was the prospect of a miracle for their friend.

So they said, "Okay, let's get him on a stretcher." They picked up the guy and got him on the stretcher. Before we move any further, here is an important thing to consider. This paralytic had accepted his situation and was in a place of complacency. I can hear him screaming, "What are you guys doing? You're hurting me. Leave me alone." Sometimes the people we are trying to help will not understand our efforts on their behalf. You must be more committed to their healing than they are.

Mark 2:3 says, "And they come unto him, bringing one sick of the palsy, which was borne of four." He was borne by four men. Each one took a corner and lifted him up. They were all involved in the task of getting their friend to Jesus. They started on the journey. The sun was bearing down on them. They were sweating. They were tired. They'd been carrying this guy for quite a while. *When will we get there?*

Finally, they were there. The house was right around the corner. They turned the corner and what did they see? The house was jammed and packed. There was no room. There was no hand-icapped zone where they could park their stretcher. No ramp to get him into the house. Now they were confronted with their next problem. How were they to maneuver through the crowd and get their friend to Jesus? Here they were, facing another obstacle.

I have discovered that the closer we get to our goals, the tougher it gets. Have you found that to be true in your own life? It seems like you're almost there. You're just about ready to step into the presence of Jesus. Just as you are ready to cross the threshold, there's always something right at the end of the journey that stands in your way.

Every occasion for success will require determination in order to succeed. Nothing good comes without much perseverance and purpose. Here is the good thing. For every problem that stands in your way, there is an answer. Nothing in the world can take the place of persistence, and persistence will bring you to the final resolution. Obstacles that stand at the door of opportunity must be opened by the hand of determination and stern resolve.

The time was urgent. Jesus did not live there. He was only visiting. They were under a time crunch and had to act quickly if they were going to walk through this open door. This is another truth that must not be missed. We don't have an unlimited amount of time to complete the tasks given to us. We cannot accept the lie that we have all the time in the world to do the divine work that has been assigned to us.

We must understand the urgency of the moment. We can't wait for others to respond. We must act, and we must act now! There is a great darkness approaching, and we have a small window of time to capture the moment. My passion for the city of New York is compounded by the crunching of time.

They knew they had to get him inside the house, and they had to get him in there quick. The house was surrounded, probably three or four deep, by a crowd of people—curious people, religious people. Now, what would they do?

Triumph Demands Tenacity

These guys did not come this far to be deterred. They were determined to complete the mission delegated to them. That's what I'm talking about! That is the kind of people I am looking for. I don't want wimps and cynics. Give me somebody who is stubborn. Give me crazy radicals who will not be detracted by obstacles and impossible situations. I don't want people who will give up in the heat of the battle. I need to have tenacious people around me, people who are committed to the task before them and will not be denied.

French chemist and microbiologist Louis Pasteur (1822-1895) had a lot of success along the way, but he also experienced a lot of failure. In looking at the success in his life, Pasteur made this observation. *Let me tell you the secret that has led me to my goal. My strength lies solely in my tenacity.*[13]

> It is easier to direct someone who is in motion than someone who is sitting on their behind.

I'd much rather have someone you need to rein in from time to time than someone who is always needing a kick in the pants to get them going. It is easier to direct someone who is in motion than someone who is sitting on their behind. There are times when I get tired of trying to motivate people to do something. I need people who have their own source of motivation. I am looking for people who are not afraid to confront the crisis and plow through to the solution.

The four friends looked at each other and wondered, *What do we do now?* Rather than being overwhelmed by the situation, they began looking for the solution. One of them noticed the flat roof over the house. *Could it work? Could we get our friend up on the roof and get him inside? That is a crazy idea. But it just might work.* Now it's one thing to carry somebody on a flat surface once you get him there. It's quite another thing to somehow haul that guy up to the roof. He was in such pain!

Not to be distracted by the impossibility of the situation, they devised a plan. Determination is good, but determination must be backed up with a good plan. Their contemplation of the situation led them to a plan. They had to get the guy to Jesus. *Why not just drop him in from the roof? It could work.*

They had a plan and now they were going to activate the plan. They pushed and they pulled as they dragged their friend up the side of the house. I can only imagine that their sick friend was screaming and hollering all the way. "What are you dong?" They tried to assure him that it would be all right. Finally, they got to the rooftop of the house. They laid their friend down. They looked for the right spot to drop him through the roof. They listened carefully until they located Jesus' voice, and then they started ripping up the roof.

Now, I don't know if you can picture that or not. But I can, perfectly. If there was anyone who would have liked to be a part of that operation, it would have been me. I love being in the middle of something that other people are saying can't be done.

I can imagine what was happening down below in the room. People were probably wondering what was going on. Straw and all kinds of dirt and dead spiders and bugs were falling down into the room.

Finally, they got a breakthrough. They saw Jesus. They walked over to their friend, grabbed the ropes they had brought with them, and begin to lower him down. As they rested him right in front of Jesus, there were smiles on their faces. *We did it. We got him to Jesus. Our task is finished.*

You must know when your task is finished. Too many people get entangled in a situation that is beyond where they should have gone. There must be balance in your life. You cannot allow your compassion to take you beyond where you should go. Get the people to Jesus and then you can back away.

Jesus Saw Their Faith

When Jesus saw their faith. That was the moment when this paralytic's life would change forever. His friends' faith created the moment for a miracle. Sometimes the miracle becomes a distraction because we miss the human side—the side of faith. It is our faith that gets us to the moment of the miracle. The Bible is a book of miracles and full of miraculous stories. Miracles are signs that God is with us and that He cares about the human dilemma. But I want to talk about the other side of miracles.

The woman with the issue of blood got healed because of her faith. (See Mark 5:25-34). Blind Bartimaeus was healed because of his faith. (See Mark 10:46-52). When the man who was born blind was told to dip into the pool of Siloam in John 9, he was healed because of his faith. The man with the withered hand in Luke 6:6 was healed because of his faith. There is the human side to the miracle.

There is a unique and interesting consideration about the paralytic's healing. He did not have faith. He was not trying to get to

Jesus. He was paralyzed by his own pain and could not fathom the possibility of ever being healed. It is possible that he had accepted his condition. He could never dream up a scenario where he would encounter God and be healed. In his mind, this sort of thing would never happen for him.

> Real faith promotes action and is the holy ground where miracles happen.

But the four friends imagined that moment—the moment when they got him to Jesus, and he was healed. What did Mark say? Mark 2:5 says, "When Jesus saw their faith." Not the cripple's faith, but the faith of his friends!

Faith is the key element in the miracle. We understand that Hebrews 11:6 is true—without faith it is impossible to please God. We need to understand that faith is more than projecting our hope into the future. Faith is about the *now*. It is acting upon God's Word today. The faith of these four men propelled them to a compassionate act. There was no reward for these four men. No promise that their *seed faith* would make them prosper. They were not looking at faith as a way to get something for themselves. They weren't gambling on God's goodness. They had faith in God's goodness.

These men had only one concern—to get this man to Jesus. Their only desire was to see their friend get the help he needed—the help they knew Jesus would give. That is faith. Faith is not passive. Faith is active. Real faith promotes action and is the holy ground where miracles happen.

Wouldn't it be nice if we were all men and women of such faith? Wouldn't the world be a better place if the Church was full of actions motivated by faith, attitudes stimulated by compassion, and work habits characterized by honesty and integrity?

These kinds of people do not need to wear a cross around their neck to mark them as Christians. Faith is their mark. There was an old book years ago. The hypothesis of the book was this. If you were ever arrested for being a Christian, would there be enough evidence against you to convict you?

"Jesus saw their faith." How did the writer of Hebrews describe faith?

> *Now faith is the substance of things hoped for, the evidence of things not seen.*
> —HEBREWS 11:1

Faith has substance to it. It is evident in our actions. Faith is not intangible, insubstantial or metaphysical. It is very real, very tangible, and very visible. Hebrews 11 lists the tangible and visible acts of the men and women of faith. They enter the halls of faith by the actions of their life. Abel made a sacrifice. Abraham left his homeland for the land of promise. Noah built a boat. Through faith they conquered kingdoms, administered justice, and gained what was promised. Through faith they shut the mouths of lions, quenched the fury of the flames, and escaped the edge of the sword. Through weakness turned into strength, they became powerful in battle and routed foreign armies.

Women received back their dead, raised to life again. Others were tortured and refused to be released so that they might gain a better resurrection. Some faced jeers and flogging, while still others were chained and put in prison. They were stoned; they were sawed in two; they were put to death by the sword. They went about in sheepskins and goatskins, destitute, persecuted and mistreated—the world was not worthy of them. They wandered in deserts and mountains, and in caves and holes in the ground. (See Hebrews 11:33-38.)

Faith without works is not faith. It's nonexistent. It is deceased. It is past. It's gone. Don't tell me about your faith until I can see it. Don't tell me that you believe God and don't act on your faith. Men and women of faith are people of action.

Faith Gets a Miracle

The four friends of the paralytic carried their friend across town. They made their way through the crowd. They pulled him up to the top of the roof. They ripped the roof apart and lowered him down to Jesus. Their job was now done. They got him to Jesus. Jesus looked up at those men and said, "Good job." When He saw their faith, He reached out to their friend and said to him, "Son, thy sins be forgiven thee."

Now, isn't that interesting? He hadn't come there to get saved. He'd been brought there to be healed. Jesus recognized that this man's first need was salvation, not healing. Before he could be healed, Jesus thought, "Let's get him saved. Let's take care of the sin problem, and then we can take care of the body problem."

As always the super spiritual folk around us can never enjoy a good miracle. They always have to complain about something. The religious leaders were infuriated with Jesus' words. *Who gave Him power to forgive men's sins? Who made Him God?* It always happens. Whenever somebody tries to do something good, there are always the detractors.

That's why He confronted the Pharisees. He would not allow them to diminish the significance of this precious moment. He confronted them with these scorching words:

> *And immediately when Jesus perceived in his spirit that they so reasoned within themselves, he said unto them, Why reason ye these things in your hearts? Whether is it easier to say to the sick of the palsy, Thy sins be forgiven thee; or to say, Arise, and take*

up thy bed, and walk? But that ye may know that the Son of man hath power on earth to forgive sins, (he saith to the sick of the palsy,) I say unto thee, Arise, and take up thy bed, and go thy way into thine house. And immediately he arose, took up the bed, and went forth before them all; insomuch that they were all amazed, and glorified God, saying, We never saw it on this fashion.

—MARK 2:8-12

Jesus looked into the eyes of those doubting theologians and said, "Watch this!" In order to convince them that He has the power to forgive, He reached out to the paralytic man and healed him in front of all who were watching this drama as it unfolded. A man with a miracle is never at the mercy of a man with an argument.

> A man with a miracle is never at the mercy of a man with an argument.

Once you come into the presence of God, you will get your miracle. He didn't need the other four anymore. Their faith had done the job. They got their friend to the Master. Now He took over and completed the task. Their dream for their friend became a reality in the presence of Jesus. This is the faith that is seen, made visible by a man's friends.

This is the kind of faith that God is looking for—if you can't see it, it isn't faith. Their faith was visible to the Lord and motivated Him to heal their friend. What did the friend do? He picked up His pallet and walked out. He didn't need his friends any more. Their job was done.

It is my prayer that the Lord will raise up a generation of young people whose faith is manifested to the world by what they do! We need visible faith, radical faith, dynamic faith that is manifested by ridiculous acts of those who trust God and believe His Word.

Chapter 4

WITH FRIENDS LIKE THIS, WHO NEEDS ENEMIES?

When we honestly ask ourselves which person in our lives means the most to us, we often find that it is those who, instead of giving much advice, solutions, or cures, have chosen rather to share our pain and touch our wounds with a gentle and tender hand. The friend who can be silent with us in a moment of despair or confusion, who can stay with us in an hour of grief and bereavement, who can tolerate not knowing, not curing, not healing and face with us the reality of our powerlessness, that is a friend who cares. [14]

A T THE BEGINNING OF time in an ancient garden God made this compelling comment: *It is not good that the man should be alone* (Genesis 2:18). And so God created a companion for Adam. It is clear that God never intended for man to live in lonely isolation. God created the first community in the Garden of Eden as a sign to future generations that friendship is a Divine idea.

Friends are our companions on our journey through this life. They laugh with us during our times of joy and they cry with us in our times of sorrow. Friends will challenge us when we are wrong and support us when we need their strength.

Not all of our associates can be counted as friends. There is a huge difference between associates and friends. The difference is usually manifested in times of trouble. Friends come in the door while others are walking out. Friends choose to listen to us in our time of need, rather than seeking to get us to draw from their potpourri of human wisdom.

Job—A Story of Suffering

One book of the Bible that is a classic story of friendship is the book of Job. Nearly every believer knows the story of Job's friends. It is the story of one man's appalling affliction and the so-called friends that tried to help him find the meaning for his suffering. As we come to the sixteenth chapter of the story, Job has had enough of these pathetic comforters and their stinging advice. With friends like these, who needs enemies?

> *Then Job answered and said, I have heard many such things: miserable comforters are ye all. Shall vain words have an end? or what emboldeneth thee that thou answerest? I also could speak as ye do: if your soul were in my soul's stead, I could heap up words against you, and shake mine head at you. But I would strengthen you with my mouth, and the moving of my lips should asswage your grief. Though I speak, my grief is not asswaged: and though I forbear, what am I eased? But now he hath made me weary: thou hast made desolate all my company. And thou hast filled me with wrinkles, which is a witness against me: and my leanness rising up in me bears witness to my face.*
> —JOB 16:1-8

In ancient times, east of Palestine, there was a man named Job who the Bible called a righteous man. Job loved God and endeavored to serve Him with all of his heart. Seeing Job's faithfulness to

Him, God rewarded him and blessed him with great riches and a wonderful family. It is at this point that the story gets interesting. This story explores the problem of suffering and where is God when it hurts. It is a true "rags to riches" account that does have a wonderful ending.

But the devil was jealous of Job's service for God and began to accuse him of only serving God because of how God had blessed him. Satan tells God that the only reason Job serves Him is because God protects him and blesses him.

Satan believes that if Job were stripped of his possessions, then Job would curse God. It is at this point that God permits Satan to go after Job. In the end Job loses all his riches, his children, and his health.

But Job does not give in, even though his wife encourages him to curse God and die! Job will not give in, and concluding this portion of the story Job pronounces his philosophy of life: God gave, and God took, blessed be the name of the Lord.

> If you find yourself in the fire or you are carrying a heavy burden, then God must trust you enough to permit these things to happen.

God trusted Job enough to allow him to go through this time of trouble. I have often said that if you find yourself in the fire or you are carrying a heavy burden, then God must trust you enough to permit these things to happen. You must be very special in the eyes of God. Usually we don't get this picture. I know this is a hard statement to accept. When you are in the circle of conflict, you often feel isolated from God's love. Believe me, I know. When I have been in the midst of a struggle, it was hard to see anything else but the trouble I was walking through.

This wasn't just a little struggle. Besides losing his wealth, he lost his kids! Only parents can understand the anguish that must have afflicted Job. He lost all ten children. There is no way that anyone could understand the deep sorrow of those days after getting the news. No parent should outlive his own children. There is no greater grief than the anguish of a parent whose child has passed away.

The final straw is the affliction that attacks Job's body. We don't know exactly what form of disease it was that overcame Job. Most Bible scholars agree that Job was stricken with some form of leprosy, maybe in a form of elephantiasis—a very dramatic form of leprosy. Whatever it was, his body was rotting away. He had boils and sores all over his body. Job 2:8 says he "took a piece of broken pottery and scraped himself with it as he sat among the ashes." He was using a potsherd to scrape away the oozing that was all over his body.

Get this picture. Here is this man who had great wealth and a wonderful family and now he is sitting in the city dump on a pile of ashes trying to get some kind of relief from the horrific pain plaguing his body. One way to think of it is to think about poison ivy. If you have had poison ivy, you will remember the intense itching and pain that you went through. Multiply that a thousand-fold and you will get a sense of what Job was experiencing.

If that is not enough, along comes his wife who tells him that he is an idiot to keep thinking that God loves him. He should give up his faith in God, curse Him and allow himself to die. What does one do in such a time of suffering? How does one combat the aching thought that just maybe God *has* forsaken you?

Job—A Story of *Helpful* Friends

Job was at the top of life and now he is at the bottom. Health gone. Children gone. Wealth gone. Wife gone. Sitting in the dump. Scraping at his flesh with a knife. How did this happen?

He is at a point in his life when a little comforting from faithful friends would be so appreciated. Friends are made for times like this.

The story of Job now takes a dramatic shift. The focus now turns to his three friends that come to see him—Eliphaz, Bilda, and Zophar. These friends have watched in silence as one disaster after another makes a deadly strike on the life of Job. They come to Job as *holy* men with a bag of theological arguments intent on convincing Job of his own sin. Their fallacious logic is typical of the self-righteous hypocrites that plague the body of Christ today.

Eliphaz, a Friend Worthy to be Heard

Eliphaz is the first to confront Job. Eliphaz was an older man and came armed with his theology of suffering. His unique logic is based on this concept: if we are suffering it is because we have sinned. He says, "Job, you have a problem and your problem is the reason why you are here. The reason why you're having these problems, the reason why you've lost your children, the reason why you've lost your wife, the reason why you're sitting here in the dump is because you have sinned. You have not had enough spiritual experiences. You're not charismatic enough. You don't speak in tongues enough. You have not had enough visions. That's why you're here." Eliphaz continues, "As a matter of fact, Job, I just had a vision last week. An angel flew right by my face and gave me goose pimples." Here is what God showed me. "God has punished you, Job, because you have sinned."

Eliphaz is rebuking Job for his pious position and because he is not willing to recognize the wisdom of the elderly. This *friend* magnifies his own spiritual experiences and seeks to present himself to Job as a person worthy to be listened to. He is a prophet of God with great wisdom and if Job would submit to him, then he would be healed. He is stunned by Job's unwillingness to submit to his godly wisdom.

Bildad, the Bible Thumper

Bildad is the next visitor to come to this guy that is "down in the dumps." As with Eliphaz he has spent a great deal of time thinking about Job's situation and has come with his own personal spin on the problem. "God is just and righteous. Job, you are so self-righteous." He is like those friends that come to us with their Bible all marked up and ready to give us some of their home-spun godly advice. I know these folk. I have heard their words before. They are the Bible thumpers. They have spent all their lives *reading* the Bible. Here is the problem. Their information is secondhand. They have knowledge, but no experience. They live their lives in a cocoon of false spirituality. I know people who worship the Bible, but have never lived the Bible.

Bildad is more concerned about Bible study than Bible living. His knowledge of the Bible exalts him above all the other folk around him. Bildad didn't care anything about winning souls. He just wanted to get deep in the Bible.

There are several things that are wrong with Bildad's approach. First, he tries to answer Job before really understanding Job. He elevates his insights without really understanding the total picture. Bildad's next problem is that his view of God is incomplete. His experiences are limited to the laboratory of theological study.

This is one of the problems with today's Bible colleges. Kids come out of those schools thinking that they know everything. They exalt knowledge over experience. These students will never be able to be the kind of friends that all of us need. They are false friends that are only seeking to correct us, rather than comfort us.

Zophar, the Dogmatic Saint

Now enters the final friend, Zophar. Zophar is a sample of the dogmatic Christian. He comes right up to Job sitting there scraping his flesh, sick, everything he once had is lost, and just needing a little love. Job gets no love from his self-righteous buddies. Zophar comes right up to Job and says, "Job, the reason why you're here, the reason why all this stuff has happened to you is because you have sin in your life." There you go. You've got to love these guys. With friends like this, you don't need any enemies.

Zophar, the fount of all wisdom, has life all figured out. The only reason why people suffer is because of sin. If people will repent, life will become good again. Let me make something real clear at this point. Nobody knows why people suffer. Some of the most wonderful Christians I have met in my life have been the people who have suffered the most. Some of the people who have lived the best lives have been those who had to endure much in this life. Suffering is a mystery. This one thing I am sure of. Suffering is not always about the sin of the sufferer.

Zophar was trying to unravel the mystery of suffering and offered this simplistic solution. It is all about sin. I wish it could be so easy. It isn't. Remember when Jesus was confronted by the Pharisees? There was a blind man near them, and they asked Jesus, "Who sinned? Was it this man or his parents?" (See John 9:2.) That was their limited understanding of suffering and sickness. Somebody had to have sinned. Jesus opened up another possibility. This man's blindness became an opportunity for the manifestation of God's glory.

If you are ever in a place of pain, never allow the pointing finger of the Pharisee to point out your sin. You need better friends than that. You don't need righteous platitudes. You just need a shoulder to lean on and some friends that can assure you of God's love and faithfulness.

Elihu, the Answer Man

The final visitor is Elihu. He is not considered one of Job's friends—just a young observer of the dialogue between Job and his friends. Elihu is a young dude full of untested knowledge. He had all the answers and was ready to test his knowledge on poor little ole Job. The wisdom of the young can be a challenge. The folly of their wisdom is that it has never been tested on the field of life. Their presumptions are weak and concocted in their private labs.

Lacking anything resembling mercy, Elihu accused Job of getting what he deserved. Elihu's focus was on the justice of God, and he challenges Job. His conclusion is that Job is in this precarious predicament because of God's judgment. The spirit constrains him to speak, even though he has no experience in life. Elihu must now vent his scorching words. He cannot restrain himself any longer.

Can you believe how much love there is in this story? Everyone wants to help Job. Their style of help is not the kind of support we need in these difficult times. Elihu displays the folly of youth. They really believe that they see things so clearly. They have not learned that the best school is the school of life. Until life has taught us, all that we have is opinions, not wisdom. And his opinions are full of holes.

> The plight of the young is that they have a tendency to overlook the wisdom of those who have gone before them.

There is much that they could learn from their elders but they choose to chart out their own paths and then will suffer the foolishness of that choice. The plight of the young is that they have a tendency to overlook the wisdom of those who have gone before them.

I have a great concern for this generation. Their music, their lifestyles, and their language are troubling. *It's no wonder some of these teenagers are so messed up. Do you know what kind of music is coming through those iPods? This so-called "music" is messed up. It's no wonder these kids speak the trash talk that comes out of their mouths. It's no wonder they treat women as they do.* I pray that God will invade this culture and turn it upside down and create an army—a holy army of young people committed to the purposes of God.

Confronting with Truth or Comforting with Love

Here is the heart of this message from the life of Job. A lot of the things these friends had to say were true. I do believe that we reap what we sow and sometimes the things we do have negative effects. I do believe that we need more experiences with God. I do believe in the justice and the judgment of God. I do believe that knowledge is important. I read and study my Bible on a regular basis.

They all had a nugget of truth in what they were saying. But they were missing something in their speeches. Job was a brother in need. He was a man who had just lost his three daughters and seven sons. He was a man whose health was lost. He didn't need to be confronted with their potion of truth. He needed to be comforted by their pockets of love. Not one of those guys came up to him and said, "Job, we're with you, brother. We care about you. What can we do to help you get through this?" No hugs and no love!

The Mark of the Christian

It is my conviction that the priority of the Church is to lift up the fallen, heal the broken and reach out to those who are lost. They don't need answers to questions they never asked. They just need a little love.

While they were there analyzing his problem…while they were there theologizing about the issue of human suffering, they should have been at Job's side praying for him and assisting him in his grief. Not one of them volunteered to sit in the dump with him. Not one of them said, "I'll stay here with you, Job, and we'll go through this thing together."

I have built my ministry on the concept that the mark of a Christian is their love, not their degree from college. Compassion is what the Church is about. That's what being a Christian is all about.

In his book, *The Mark of a Christian,* the renowned American Evangelical Christian theologian, philosopher and Presbyterian pastor Francis Schaeffer (1912-1984) put it this way.

"My children, I will be with you only a little longer. You will look for me, and just as I told the Jews, so I tell you now: Where I am going, you cannot come. A new command I give you: Love one another. As I have loved you, so you must love one another. By this all men will know that you are my disciples, if you love one another" (John 13:33-35 NIV).

This passage reveals the mark that Jesus gives to label a Christian not just in one era or in one locality but at all times and all places until Jesus returns. Notice that what he says here is not a description of a fact. It is a command, which includes a condition: 'A new command I give you: Love one another. As I have loved you, so you must love one another. By this all men will know that you are my disciples, if you love one another.' An **if** is involved. **If** you obey, you will wear the badge Christ gave. But since this is a command, it can be violated.

The point is that it is possible to be a Christian without showing the mark, but if we expect non-Christians to know that we are Christians, we must show the mark."[15]

It is my conviction that we should eliminate the kind of Christianity that simply points a finger at the lost and hurting and says, "You're a sinner. You're out of the will." We should marginalize those Christians who are not willing to lift up people who are in the valley of pain. It is critical that we understand that the best way to reach the world is to get out of the security of our cloistered communities and get into the places where people are desperate for our love and support. That is real Christianity.

I remember a few years ago when I was in Florida. I was driving down Ninth Street in St. Petersburg where I lived. It was about one o'clock in the morning, and I was on a winding road and came to a corner. Looking ahead, I saw a Mustang convertible that had hit a tree head-on. There were two people in the front and one in the back. One of the persons in the backseat had been flung out of the car. They had to have been going about 100 miles an hour. I got out of my car and rushed to this tragic scene. One of the persons in the back had been impaled by a tree limb. I used to race cars, but I have never seen anything this bad on the racetrack.

When I came on that wreck, I did not run up to those who were still in the car and say, "Hey, whose fault is this? Is it yours? Do you believe the book of Revelation? Are you a premillenialist or a post millenialist? Do you smoke?"

I didn't do that! What did I do? There was somebody there who needed help and without even thinking, I began to act on their behalf. I remember thinking, "By the help and grace of God, I'm going do something to help these people."

Once again, allow me to be clear! I am not saying that we should not preach against sin. I am not saying that we should not study our Bibles. I am not saying there is something wrong with spiritual experiences. What I am saying is this: all of this is irrelevant if it is done in exclusion to reaching out to a world that is hopeless and desperate for love and comfort.

> I have built this ministry in the inner city in order to lift up the downtrodden, to reach out to the hopeless, and to care for those who have been disenfranchised by poverty, crime and abuse.

I didn't buy buses to bring kids to Sunday School so that I could flaunt my ministry and show people what I am doing. I did it because I care for these kids. I could do nothing else. The compassion that motivates my life constrains me to reach out to them and embrace them with the love of God. I have built this ministry in the inner city in order to lift up the downtrodden, to reach out to the hopeless, and to care for those who have been disenfranchised by poverty, crime and abuse.

We have a city that's full of people like Job. There are neighborhoods that are dying and longing for someone to care. Too many people in my city are more concerned about building their ministry than building up people. We have too many people more interested in building fancy buildings and attracting the rich than they are in creating a place where people can have their needs met. Jesus made it clear in His Word what was the focus of His ministry.

> *The Spirit of the Lord is upon me, because he hath anointed me to preach the gospel to the poor; he hath sent me to heal the brokenhearted, to preach deliverance to the captives, and recovering of sight to the blind, to set at liberty them that are bruised, to preach the acceptable year of the Lord.*
>
> —LUKE 4:18-19

I don't fantasize about the platforms that I have stood upon and the sermons I have preached. I don't glory in all of the places that I have flown to over the years. Here is what I remember. I remember the people who I have seen delivered from drugs. I remember the people who have been saved from child abuse. I remember the poor who have been fed. I remember the smiles on the faces of those kids as they open up the Christmas gifts that we have given them. That is what I remember.

I remember when a pastor friend of mine came to visit us. He spoke these words to me. "You don't know this, but one of the reasons why I brought a work crew to fix up the building down here is…" He continued with these heartfelt words, "When you came to my church five years ago, we were facing a major split. I was scared. I didn't know what to do." As his face was gleaming with joy, he explained, "but you came and preached a sermon on David and Goliath, called 'Nurtured in Solitude, Strengthened in Conflict, Proven in Hopelessness.'" He finished the story by telling me that he took that sermon and he made it his own because it had empowered him to face his own situation.

It spoke to his heart and gave him comfort and strength. In his office is a plaque about the size of my Bible, and on that plaque is my sermon outline that I preached that day. I didn't know it at the time, but I had become a true friend to him. I had lifted him up out of his despair and given him the power to navigate through those treacherous waters and bring his church back to a place of healing.

I remember the day when I got a phone call from an Assembly of God pastor. Listening to him, he began to relate this story. "I can't tell this to anybody. I hope you're for real." He continued with this amazing story. "Within an hour the FBI will be at my house. Somebody in the church is trying to set me up. There's been a murder in our area and the description of the murderer fits my profile.

"Somebody, one of my enemies, has set me up. The FBI is coming to interrogate me on suspicion of murder!" With sadness in his voice, he related, "I've got three kids, man. I didn't do it. What am I gonna tell those guys?" With deep and genuine concern, I told this guy, "You hang in there, buddy. You hang in there. God will help you. God will vindicate you, but you hang in there." I said, "Don't give up. Don't give up! Don't give up."

There is no substitute for sitting down with somebody and putting your arm around them, and telling them how much you care. It has been my goal to motivate my staff with this kind of compassion. On one Christmas, I was in my office and most of the staff was gone. It was about 8:30 P.M. One last staff member came into my office and said that they needed to go visit someone. Looking up at them I asked, "Where are you going?" He said, "Somebody on my bus route, a little ten-year-old boy, is in Elmhurst Hospital tonight. He tried to commit suicide. He's in the lock-up at Elmhurst."

With words of compassion, she continued, "I just want to go see him. It's Christmas Eve. I just want him to know that someone cares." What was she trying to do? Lift him up. Lift him up. No one will ever know that she performed this act of kindness. She will never tell others how great she was. No! She only had one concern. She just wanted this little boy to know that on this Christmas Eve, there was someone thinking about him. He was not alone.

That is true friendship. That is the kind of love that is the mark of the true Christian. The world doesn't need the friendship of Job's self-righteous friends. They need the love of someone who truly cares and will lift them up out of their sorry state and give them a reason for living. It is this kind of Christianity that will restore the reputation of the Church in a world of hurting people.

Chapter 5

THE FRIENDSHIP TEST

A doubtful friend is worse than a certain enemy. Let a man be one thing or the other, and we then know how to meet him.[16]

FRIENDS ARE LIKE ROSES; you have to be careful of the thorns. Even the strongest friendship can be transformed into a nightmare. They can turn on a dime at any moment and leave us alone and forsaken. A friend's words, if we are not careful, can lead us into perilous places. Not all friends are good for you. Friendships are so important in our lives, but if we choose the wrong friends, they can be detrimental and place us at risk.

No matter how you look at it, the people you spend time with have a huge influence on your life. I have watched people enter our program, and they are such wonderful people when they come to us. But if they get in with the wrong group, they end up becoming polluted by the negativity of those influences.

You will be known by the company you keep and those you allow into the living room of your life can have disastrous effects. "Put a rose in a sack of fish and soon the rose will start to stink too. Be careful of the company you keep."[17]

You know idiots attract idiots. Solomon had it right when he wrote these words in Proverbs 30:15—*The horseleach hath two daughters, crying, Give, give. There are three things that are never satisfied, yea, four things say not, It is enough.* Every bloodsucker has others that are ready to suck the lifeblood out of you. It's sad, but it is true. You must beware of the associations that you create in your life. You must be cautious of the people who are trying to sneak into your life.

Bad Friends Corrupt

There is a story in the time of David that illustrates my point—judge your friends wisely!

> *And it came to pass after this, that Absalom the son of David had a fair sister, whose name was Tamar; and Amnon the son of David loved her. And Amnon was so vexed, that he fell sick for his sister Tamar; for she was a virgin; and Amnon thought it hard for him to do anything to her. But Amnon had **a friend**, whose name was Jonadab, the son of Shimeah David's brother: and Jonadab was a very subtil man. And he said unto him, Why art thou, being the king's son, lean from day to day? wilt thou not tell me? And Amnon said unto him, I love Tamar, my brother Absalom's sister. And Jonadab said unto him, Lay thee down on thy bed, and make thyself sick: and when thy father cometh to see thee, say unto him, I pray thee, let my sister Tamar come, and give me meat, and dress the meat in my sight, that I may see it, and eat it at her hand.*
>
> —2 SAMUEL 13:1-5

This story of two of King David's children—Amnon and Tamar—and Amnon's cousin and friend, Jonadab, is truly a tragic one and a perfect example of why it's important to choose your friends wisely. Yes, I said cousin **and friend.** Amnon's dad was Shimeah, David's brother.

If you are at all familiar with the Old Testament, you know that as a young warrior, David had enjoyed the comfort and security of having a really close friend, King Saul's son, Jonathan. David knew intimately the benefits to be enjoyed by having a faithful and trustworthy friend. Jonathan and David were as close as brothers—perhaps closer than some brothers—and probably closer than David was to Amnon's dad. Amnon, David's son, should have realized the importance of a good friend by observing the friendship that had existed between his father and Jonathan.

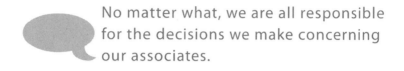

No matter what, we are all responsible for the decisions we make concerning our associates.

Amnon did not get that message. He chose Jonadab. It was a really bad decision. No matter what, we are all responsible for the decisions we make concerning our associates. If we end up choosing bad companions, we will pay a price for that decision and be held accountable. We are responsible for those choices and the risky consequences that accompany them.

It is clear that these two guys spent a lot of time together, and I am sure that Amnon had told Jonadab about his lustful desires toward his stepsister. One translation of 2 Samuel 13:3 calls Jonadab, "a very crafty friend." Amnon should have known that his desires were wrong, and he should have never opened his heart to his friend. But he did, and the crafty Jonadab planted the seeds of destruction in his friend's heart.

It's a weird, kinky story—a son of the great King David falling in love with his stepsister! All of the battles we wage in life are won or lost in the mind. Jonadab introduced the thought, and Amnon fed on it to his own destruction. Jonadab spoke his poisonous words: "Amnon, you are obsessed with this girl. Heck, it's even making you sick, you're so in love with her! Here's the plan. When everybody is gone, you stay home. Fake like you're sick. Get your dad to tell her to make you some food. Then when she comes into your room, then you make your move." The thought leads to a plan. The plan is hatched and leads to an insidious act of rape.

A good friend would have countered Amnon's lustful thoughts by challenging him to think better about his stepsister. A really good friend would have been appalled by even the suggestion of a brother lusting after his stepsister and expressed his alarm that such a thought had ever entered Amnon's mind! He should have said, "Get up out of that bed, Stupid! Stop this nonsense right now over a girl who is clearly off limits to you! What an idiot! We have to get your mind on something else. Let's play ball!" But not Amnon. He chose the wrong friend and Jonadab became a co-conspirator in this appalling story.

Remember when God told Abraham to take his son and sacrifice him on Mount Moriah? Abraham obeyed God and left early the next morning. When they got to the bottom of the mountain, Genesis 22:5 says, "Abraham said to his young men, Abide ye here with the ass [donkey]; and I and the lad will go over yonder and worship, and come again to you." Before he took Isaac to complete the journey, it says he left his friends there. Why did he do that? Do you have any idea? Why did he leave his friends at the bottom of the mountain?

Abraham knew what he must do and he could not trust these friends. With their good intentions they would try to stop him. He did not need this kind of advice. He needed to be free to do what God called him to do without the counsel of his friends. Do not be deceived: "Bad company corrupts good morals." (See 1 Corinthians 15:33.)

Please listen to me! I don't know who you're spending time with, but you had better pick them real carefully. Your life depends upon it. I pick my friends very carefully. That's why I have very few. I understand that the people who are close to me must be people of similar vision and passion. I cannot allow knuckleheads to be in my inner circle. I aggressively protect that place. People might think that I am aloof, but they do not understand the value that I place on good friends.

Too Much Time With Friends—A Bad Thing

It is possible to spend too much time with your friends. If you are not careful you will find yourself drifting into gossip or negative talk that can result in all kinds of negativity. Once you start wandering into discussions about other people, if you are not careful, you will find yourself in caustic gossip. You can only talk about good stuff for so long. I don't care how good a friend you have, you are limited on how long you can stay positive.

That's why I hate going out to eat after Sunday morning church with the staff. I hate it. I'm trying to come up with a reason to get out of it without looking like a complete party pooper. If we're not careful, we end up in this kind of dialog, "Did you hear what that person did?" "Can you believe they said that?" "What do you think about this person?"

> Loyalty is refusing to be drawn into disparaging discussions about other people.

I remember one time when the pastor of a church got mad at me. I was simply trying to protect him when I scolded one of his board members—which I must say I enjoyed doing. He was being very critical of the pastor, and I just could not stand it any longer and gave him a tongue lashing on the danger of criticizing leadership.

Dis-loyalty is 'dissing' those you should be loyal to. Loyalty is refusing to be drawn into disparaging discussions about other people. That is disloyalty. If you hear somebody criticizing your friend or a leader at any level and you don't stand up and say something, as far as I'm concerned, you are guilty of disloyalty.

Because this is a principle that guides my life, I have preachers from all over the world who trust me. They know I won't betray them by talking to others. I don't sit in the "Green Room" talking about other preachers. There are enough people who do that. We don't need one more. We don't need it in Christianity.

There is no good that comes out of criticizing others. All it does is tear down the other person and split relationships. Rather than criticizing people, we should be encouraging them. Rather than lusting after others, we should be praying for them.

It doesn't matter where you are in life, there will always be bad friends knocking on your door. The key to life is in never opening that door. It doesn't matter who they are because it will come back to bite you. All betrayal begins with trust and that is why you must always be careful whom you trust. Never say anything in private that you can't say in public. If a friendship is broken, your words just might be put on the public stage.

To this day I am still dealing with the problems created by some of the folk who came to work in this ministry. No matter how many people I have working for me and no matter how carefully we screen them, bad apples always seem to appear. Once I find them, they are gone! You will be known for two things in life: the problems you solve and the problems you create.

The people near you must be tested. You must know that they can be counted on and that they are true friends. Here are some tests that will help you weed out the bad seed in your life.

The Friendship Test # 1—Does Your Friend Encourage You to Do Right or Wrong?

All of us have different levels of friendships—our friends at work, at church, and in our neighborhood. These friendships are categorized by the degree to which we share our lives with them. Success in your friendships is developed by your ability to identify the people you can trust.

What kind of friends do you have? Do you put your friends to the test? A friend who encourages you to do wrong is not a friend. How do they handle the secrets of your life? Are they there when you need them? Are they willing to challenge you when you are going in the wrong direction?

I have discovered that you can eventually find somebody who will listen to you and will encourage you to keep heading down a dark path. That's what happened with Amnon and Jonadab. You have to ask yourself whether you have a Jonathan or a Jonadab in your life. Your friends will reflect your values. Those you hang out with create a brand on your life. If you hang out with idiots, people will brand you as an idiot.

Another son of David, Solomon, philosophically put it this way: "The righteous should choose his friends carefully, for the way of the wicked leads them astray" (Proverbs 12:26 NKJV). Pick your friends wisely lest they become a *distraction* for you and a *misrepresentation* of you. If your friend is not leading you or is not encouraging you or is not motivating you or is not helping you to get closer to God, you had better drop that person right now.

The Friendship Test # 2—Does Your Friend Encourage You to Do Something Against Your Family?

Friends who encourage you to do something they know will hurt your family are not your friends. This test can apply to either your biological family or your spiritual family. You need to run from anyone who seeks to break your relationship with your family or advises you to do evil to your family!

Jonadab encouraged Amnon to rape his stepsister. How weird is that? What kind of a friend is that? This is an extreme case, but believe me, there are some weird people in this world who will seek to seduce us to do wrong.

 A person's character will be tested by the kind of people he invites into his life.

If those people become negative influences—either seeking or causing you to do wrong to your family—you are in trouble. They have failed the friendship test and are not your friends. A person's character will be tested by the kind of people he invites into his life.

The Friendship Test # 3—Does Your Friend Encourage You to Lie?

A friend who encourages you to lie is not your friend. Lying is a fruit of doing something wrong. When we have transgressed, we lie to cover up our transgressions. The problem with lying is that you will always get caught, even if you are a President. Someone said that lying is like alcoholism; you are always recovering. Once you start lying, you cannot stop. It becomes an addiction. A person who seeks to get you to lie is a dealer in falsehoods and endeavoring to ensnare you in their own little web.

A lie is destructive and runs at the speed of light. American author and humorist Mark Twain (1835-1910) once said that a lie has traveled half way around the world while the truth is still putting on its shoes. You cannot recover a lie. It is always there in the back of a person's mind. Lies ensnare. Lies deceive. Lies betray. Lies hurt. Lies live forever! Do not be a friend of liars.

The Friendship Test # 4—Does Your Friend Encourage You to be Immoral?

Jonadab encouraged Amnon to be immoral with his stepsister. What a friend! He convinced him to rape his sister. Desperate people will do desperate things. Amnon was driven to desperation by his lust and Jonadab assisted him in his delusions. Some people are so desperate to have friends that they will settle for the wrong people. Let me make this point clear. *It's better to be alone than to be with the wrong person!* It is better to remain alone than to choose the wrong people and watch that decision destroy your family, your ministry, and your life.

I know what it means to be lonely, but I have chosen to be lonely rather than have the wrong people in my life. I have counted the cost. Desperate people will end up in the wrong bed with the wrong person.

Amnon's desperation got him killed. It took two years, but it happened. When Absalom found out what his stepbrother Amnon had done to his sister, he was furious. He waited for just the right time and killed him. You will never get away with your sin. It will find you. Two years, two weeks, two months, two days, or twenty years later, you will get caught.

Here's the crazy part of the story. Do you know who told David that his son Amnon had been killed? It was this stellar nephew of his Jonadab! Isn't that interesting? Amnon is dead, and Jonadab gets off *scot-free*. Webster defines the term *scot-free* as "free from obligation, harm, punishment, or penalty." Jonadab is in the background sowing his seeds of destruction and watches while Amnon is killed!

Choose your friends carefully. Men and women of God must be extremely careful about the kinds of people who surround them. There are only a handful of people that I allow into the inner sanctuary of my life. I test those who want to be my friend. They are qualified by their words and their actions. I don't have time to engage in frivolous relationships. I must make every moment of my life count. I am on a mission, and I want people around me who can support that cause.

And so it should be in your life. You had better test the people around you. You had better make sure they are real friends. Choose your friends wisely!

Chapter 6

HE'S THE GOD OF THE HILLS AND THE VALLEYS

As the valley gives height to the mountain, so can sorrow give meaning to pleasure; as the well is the source of the fountain, deep adversity can be a treasure.[18]

LIFE IS FULL OF peaks and valleys. No one lives forever on the mountaintop and, thank God, no one lives forever in the valley. But both places are important to the building of character and vision in our lives. Strength, courage and integrity are built into our lives in the valley seasons of life, and they are tested as we enjoy success on the mountaintop. Things look bigger in the valley, and they look smaller at the peak. Vision is sharpened in the valley and expanded on the mountain.

The seasoned veterans among us have learned that God is with us in the valley and on the mountain. We are not forsaken. He is God of both the hills and the valleys. This is the lesson that we learn in the story found in the Old Testament.

> *Their gods are gods of the hills; therefore they were stronger than we; but let us fight against them in the plain, and surely we shall be stronger than they. And do this thing, Take the kings away, every man out of his place, and put captains in their rooms: And number thee an army, like the army that thou hast*

lost, horse for horse, and chariot for chariot: and we will fight against them in the plain, and surely we shall be stronger than they. And he hearkened unto their voice, and did so. And it came to pass at the return of the year, that Benhadad numbered the Syrians, and went up to Aphek, to fight against Israel. And the children of Israel were numbered, and were all present, and went against them: and the children of Israel pitched before them like two little flocks of kids; but the Syrians filled the country. And there came a man of God, and spake unto the king of Israel, and said, Thus saith the LORD, Because the Syrians have said, The LORD is God of the hills, but he is not God of the valleys, therefore will I deliver all this great multitude into thine hand, and ye shall know that I am the LORD. And they pitched one over against the other seven days. And so it was, that in the seventh day the battle was joined: and the children of Israel slew of the Syrians an hundred thousand footmen in one day.

—1 KINGS 20:23-29

God of the Valleys and God of the Hills

The Syrians were a force to be reckoned with. Their first king was Benhadad I, named after the Syrian god, Hadad (god of the storm). From Damascus, their capital in western Asia, Benhadad II gathered together his army, augmented by the induction of the armies of 32 local chieftains. They marched toward Samaria and after a siege to the capital they conquered the Samaritans. Samaria was built on about a 300-foot high mountain. His ultimate goal was to defeat the armies of Israel. He had already lost a battle against Israel in the mountains. His astrologers were telling him that the God of Israel is the God of the mountains. So, their advice was to attack Israel in the valley.

This is a powerful truth. Remember the story of Job that we already reviewed a while back? Satan challenged God, telling Him that if he (Satan) were allowed to attack Job, then old Job would give up his faith in God. That is still the enemy's strategy. If he can bring trouble into the lives of God's people, they will abandon their faith. Unfortunately, these devilish attacks have worked on a lot of God's people. We love God when we are on the mountaintop, enjoying His blessings and favor.

But when we get into the valley, we become a bunch of whiners wondering why God has forsaken us. The gospel of prosperity, so prominent in this generation, has not prepared us to endure in the valley of trouble. I've seen churches destroyed. I've seen ministries destroyed. And I've seen families destroyed because people do not have the survival skills to help them endure in the low places.

> Teflon rhinos are equipped to survive prosperity and to endure hardship.

Teflon rhinos know that God is the God of the valley, as well as God of the mountain. They know how to successfully live in both places. They are equipped to survive prosperity and to endure hardship. They know that there is a purpose for the hill, a potential in the valley, and a press of living between these two worlds.

We all love life on the hill! Living in the blessing and favor of God is a wonderful thing. Life at the top is a place of success, miracles and strength. When God comes to visit us, we all enjoy basking in His glory. His presence is so real, His power so dynamic, and everything we do seems to prosper. But that does not last forever.

> The person who does not perceive the purposes of pain will not succeed in life.

Most of us get confused when we get into the valley. We don't understand *why* these things have happened. We become confused when sorrow overtakes our joy, when trouble trumps our ease, and sickness challenges our health. Why? That is the question I want to answer in this chapter. If we are to outlive our problems in the valley, we must understand their purpose. There is purpose in the valley, and the person who does not perceive the purposes of pain will not succeed in life.

The goal of life is learning how to be abased and how to abound. The apostle Paul said in Philippians 4:12-13, "I know both how to be abased, and I know how to abound: every where and in all things I am instructed both to be full and to be hungry, both to abound and to suffer need. I can do all things through Christ which strengtheneth me." If we are to thrive in this life, we must learn to live in the press between the hill and the mountain.

Purpose of the Hill—Define Your Cause

The hilltop helps you to define your vision and determine your cause. It is in those times that I want to emphasize again how important it is to be careful about the people who surround you. The people who surround you will have an affect upon the things that you see—they will weigh in on how you see things. Their vision and perception of life will have an impact upon you.

Men and women must be careful about who they marry because you are marrying into the other person's vision and purpose. Two cannot walk together unless they are in agreement (see Amos 3:3).

If you marry into the wrong vision, you are setting yourself up for a great deal of trouble.

In times of revival the glory of God is so real and relevant. When we are living in the manifest presence of God, our vision is sharpened so that we can understand the cause of God in our times. Leaving the valley of smog where vision is clouded and purpose is confusion, we attempt to ascend into the unpolluted atmosphere of God's presence. In those high places we are able to see further than we could ever see in the valley. God took Moses up into the high places of Mount Sinai and showed him His glory. Jesus took His disciples up to the top of the Mount of Transfiguration and they were able to see who He really was.

There is something about the high places that sharpens our vision and refines our purpose. Away from the clouds and mists that exist in the low places, we are able to see terrain that we have never seen before. We gain perspective that we never had.

The mountaintop lets you see life, people, circumstances and the will of God in ways that we never have seen before. If you don't climb the mountain, you can't see the plain. You see clearer and farther on the mountain.

In describing what it was like to discover a new theory, Albert Einstein put it in these words: *Creating a new theory is not like destroying an old barn and erecting a skyscraper in its place. It is rather like climbing a mountain, gaining new and wider views, discovering unexpected connections between our starting points and its rich environment. But the point from which we started out still exists and can be seen, although it appears smaller and forms a tiny part of our broad view gained by the mastery of the obstacles on our adventurous way up.*[19]

You come to a higher place when you to enter into worship, for example. You enter into the shift that God is doing with us in order to win. I'm not trying to get you to be overly spiritual. I'm not interested in that. I'm trying to get you to enter in so you can come to a higher place and see, have a clear vision, a clearer direction of where you need to go from where you are today. If you're in business or in ministry, perhaps you are seeking God to know to what level your department needs to go or if you are in ministry, where your ministry is going. That is the purpose of the mountaintop.

The mountaintop experience is for one purpose, to bring you up so you can see clearly. You become aware of your gifts and potential. You see the future and all that it holds for you. Your eyes are opened to see things you have never noticed before. Your heart is encouraged, your mind is enlightened, and your life is strengthened. Once we get away from the predicaments presented in the valleys, we are able to think without the encroaching issues posed by people and problems.

Potential of the Valley—Destroys Your Clarity

When you descend from the mountain, you are confronted with all kinds of issues that can destroy the clarity that you gained on the mountain. The potential of the valley is likely destruction. When Moses came down from Mount Sinai, he was confronted by a golden calf. When the disciples came down from the Mount of Transfiguration, a demon-possessed person who they could not deliver challenged them. Descending into the valley will always present a set of problems that will defy what you have witnessed on the mountaintop.

 Our valley experiences can and usually do cause us to become very vulnerable.

Danger waits for you in the valley. Down here the highs are very high and the lows are very low. It's an emotional upheaval. If you are not prepared for the lows of the valley, you will be in trouble. If you're not spiritually and emotionally prepared for that, you will struggle and you won't make it. Our valley experiences can and usually do cause us to become very vulnerable.

The enemy will not attack you *with* a valley. We think we come under attack, and the enemy attacks us with a valley. No, no! He attacks you while you're *in* the valley. The things you encounter in the valley are not the issue. The problem is how you react to those things.

Nobody quits while they are on the mountain! The temptation to give up is always lurking at our side as we walk through the darkness in the valley. When we get sick, lose our job, have problems in our marriage, or are betrayed by someone we believed was a friend, these are the moments of decision. How will we react? Will we give in to depression? Will we get angry? Will we run away?

It is while we are in the valley that the friends like Job come out of the cracks to feed us their recipe of guilt, condemnation and judgment. It is while we are down in the dumps that each of us is susceptible to depression and failure. Our vision is dimmed. Then our strength is sapped. Our joy is trampled upon. How quickly life can change! In the blink of an eye, our world can tumble upside down.

The potential of the valley to crush your vision is a very real thing. It is the nature of the world we live in. Valleys happen to all of us, and they blur our vision. It is in those moments when our vision is impaired that we must not give in to the despair and anger and pain.

The Press in Between Develops Your Character

Life is lived in between the mountain and the valley. There is a pressure in between those two places. All of us have to come to see that there is a purpose in the process. It is the process that connects the dream to the reality. It is in the process that character is developed. Character is not a gift. Character is the result of what we learn and experience in life. Character develops itself in the stream of life, a stream that flows from the mountain to the valley.

All of us rejoice when we discover our purpose. We are enthralled with the vision that comes to us on the mountaintop. We must also understand that it is the process that makes the dream a reality. Too many dreams have been forfeited in the valley of disappointment and heartache.

We are people of destiny, and we must understand that any dark cloud that overshadows that destiny is only a shadow. The dark clouds will pass. Be careful that you do not miss your purpose while you are walking through the process. The process is the only way to reach your destiny.

I am not a masochist. I don't like pain. But I do know that pain is part of the process that brings us to our destiny. There is no one there to open the door for you. You must open that door yourself. You can't depend on others to get you through the valley. You have to plot out your own course. Character and strength are developed as you press forward, choosing not to look behind you. This is no time to glance in your rear-view mirror.

When I was younger, my highs were very high and my lows were very low. I may have been schizophrenic, I don't know, but I would be enjoying the heights of glory and then when the bottom fell from under my feet, I would freak out. I have discovered through the process that you cannot allow the highs and lows to destroy you. Now I try to find the balance in all things—not too high and not too low.

You're only as strong as you are when you are at your weakest. Character is not necessarily *built* in the valley, but it is *manifested* in the valley. What are you like when you are down? I am not impressed with people's strength when they are on the mountain, but I am impressed with people's resolve when life has slapped them in the face.

Don't tell me you have a great marriage on your honeymoon. Talk to me after you have been married for ten years. Don't tell me about your great revelation and the miracles you have performed and the great sermons you have preached. Preach your sermon to me when you are walking through hell. Then I will listen.

What do you do when you are in the valley? You keep moving. You get out of bed every morning. You put your feet on the floor, and then you put one foot in front of the other. You do not give up. If you keep moving, eventually you will come out of the valley. There is a morning for every night season. Sorrow will eventually be replaced with joy. Pain will be substituted with healing.

Hebrews 13:5 says, "I will never leave you, nor forsake you..." In the Greek language it is a quintupled negative. The writer is saying that God will never, not never, no never, or ever forsake you. I love how the Amplified Bible says it, "...for He [God] has said, I will not in any way fail you nor give you up nor leave you without support. [I will] not, [I will] not in any degree leave you helpless nor forsake nor let [you] down (relax My hold on you)! [Assuredly not!]"

Wow! We do not take the valley walk alone. Just as His presence is so obvious on the mountain, so it is just as real in the valley. Others might forsake you, but He will never, ever forsake you. His presence might not be felt like it is on the mountain, but He is there to give you strength to keep moving on.

I don't know about you, but I am not going back. I am not going back. I will not allow myself to regress in life. I will not give up the ground that I have gained. Let the enemy throw all that he has against me. I know that my strength is in the Lord, and I can sustain the heaviest onslaught the enemy throws against me.

Isaiah 59:19 says, "When the enemy shall come in like a flood, the Spirit of the Lord shall lift up a standard against him." Your destiny is not in a valley. It is only a place of transition to get you back on track and headed toward the next mountain. You are moving from one mountain of glory to the next, punctuated by valley times.

The process is designed to get you from where you are to where you need to be. Don't let that valley keep bringing you down. Remember those immortal words from Dr. Martin Luther King's speech, "I Have a Dream."

> *"I have a dream that one day every valley shall be exalted, every hill and mountain shall be made low, the rough places will be made straight and the glory of the Lord shall be revealed and all flesh shall see it together."* [20]

Chapter 7

VICTORY IN THE VALLEYS

One sees great things from the valley and only small things from the peak.[21]

THE VALLEY IS A place of testing. A person might be wonderfully gifted, but those gifts do not necessarily make you a leader in difficult times. Gifted people can open doors by virtue of their skills and abilities, but it takes character to survive and inhabit the room. I know people who have had powerful gifts but further down the road, they are no longer in leadership.

That is one of the problems of today's education, both secular and spiritual. We give people information, but we do not prepare them for life. They think that it is their learning that equips them to fulfill their future roles. It is in difficult times that our character is tested and our education is no guarantee that we will pass the test. It is in the valley of trouble that our real nature is unveiled.

A gifted person will call people to their side but a tested person will get people to remain at their side. How you act in the times of dilemma and difficulty defines your leadership. That's why leadership in today's society is all fouled up, because they're either appointed or they're elected. Appointed leadership and elected leadership really isn't leadership at all. Biblical leadership is discovered when men and women arise with power and a plan in challenging times.

In some ways people determine the leader by the decision to follow that leader. A position does not determine leadership. It is what you do with that position that will verify your leadership capabilities. There is nothing so annoying as a leader who cannot communicate his vision in critical times. It is vision that attracts people. People will cross the line and hitch their wagon to a person of vision in the complicated and dangerous cycles of life.

Vision is one of the key ingredients for success in the valley. Vision must be clearly delineated and forcefully carried out. Leadership is not a popularity contest. That is one of the weaknesses of democracy. Just because a person is elected does not mean he can lead.

Leadership demands tough decisions that go against the grain of public opinion. It sounds great when a ministry says they have 186 different ministries. A leader's vision is focused and firmed, not dependent on pleasing the people. Where is this leadership uncovered? It is in the valley. At some point all leaders will be tested and that test will prove the precision of their vision and the strength of their character.

A Presence in the Valley

Yea, though I walk through the valley of the shadow of death,
I will fear no evil: for thou art with me.

—PSALM 23:4

One of the keys to valley survival is in knowing that there is a *Presence* that is with you in the valley—a *Divine Presence.* "Thou art with me"—four powerful words from the Psalmist who was intimately acquainted with the valleys as well as the mountaintop experiences. There is nothing so wonderful as knowing that you are not alone. When the battle emerges, the tendency for most people is to run. Courage is a rare commodity among the human race. The battle weeds out cowards and leaves the courageous in lonely places. What a powerful thing it is to know that even though all have gone AWOL at one time or another, we are *never* alone. God walks with us as death casts its daunting shadow over our lives.

Theology instructs us that God is omnipresent—present everywhere at the same moment. But theological explanations will not be helpful in the valley. What we need to be confident in is that God is with us! Biblical leadership is certain in that truth. They know that God is *with* them and *in* them. God is supporting them and God is strengthening them.

> The Divine presence is key to surviving as you make your trek through the valleys of life.

I have probably spent three quarters of my life in the valley. I am a connoisseur of fine valleys, because I've been in them so much. I have had to struggle, fight and overcome many obstacles to get to this place in life. The people who have watched my life have been astonished that I am still standing. I have been shot at, betrayed, criticized and ridiculed, but I refuse to give up. I know that though others forsake me, God will never forsake me. I have learned the essence of His presence. It is more than something I *know*. It is something that I have *experienced* in the darkest times of my life.

How do you get through these valleys? The Bible talks a lot about valleys. Valleys represent dark times, difficult times and times of death. It is only the people of character who know that God is with them who will survive those epoch seasons in their lives.

Valley of Kidron—*Valley of Suffering*

The valley of Kidron is now called the valley of Jehosophat and is just outside the eastern gate of the city of Jerusalem. It is actually in very close proximity to the Garden of Gethsemane. The Kidron

Valley runs along the eastern wall of the Old City of Jerusalem, separating the Temple Mount from the Mount of Olives. It then continues east through the Judean Desert toward the Dead Sea.[22]

What kind of valley is the Valley of Kidron? It represents the valley of suffering. The Valley of Kidron was once a cemetery. Absalom was buried there. Samson and Samuel were buried there. I know a few things about the valley of suffering. I have walked that path many times in my life. If you have not suffered, you have not visited the Valley of Kidron.

Suffering has nothing to do with faith. No amount of faith will prevent you from walking through this valley. Don't let any preacher deceive you. We will all pass by that valley. Faith is a gift that enables you to *survive* in the valley of suffering, not to *prevent* you from passing through.

I am an observer of people's lives and I have watched how people handle tragedy. You get a phone call and calamity slaps you in the face. You are never prepared for those moments. The phone rings and you find out that your child was killed in a car wreck. You are called into your employer's office and are stunned when you find out that you have been fired. Welcome to the Valley of Kidron. Everything changes when you step into that valley. Your joy is destroyed. Your peace is rattled. Your strength is sapped. Your faith is challenged.

The salvation of the world is in the hands of those who have suffered. This is the principle of the cross. God was willing to suffer in order to bring salvation to the lost human race. It is a divine principle of life that cannot be denied. Our future leaders are somewhere walking through the Valley of Kidron, being developed for their future task.

How do you get through the valley of suffering? You allow yourself to be impelled forward by a Divine Force.

Suffering is a passageway to a new life—a changed life. Henry Drummond (1851-1897), a Scottish evangelist, writer and lecturer, in his book *The Changed Life,* used one of the laws of motion to describe how our lives are changed. "Every body continues in its state of rest, or of uniform motion in a straight line, except in so far as it may be compelled by impressed forces to change that state. This is also a first law of Christianity. Every man's character remains as it is, or continues in the direction in which it is going, until it is compelled by impressed forces to change that state."[23] Suffering is an impressed force that pushes you into places you would never choose. But there can never be legitimate and significant change without going through the Valley of Kidron.

How do you get through the valley of suffering? When your heart has been ripped out of your body, what do you do? You push forward. You allow yourself to be impelled forward by the Divine Force.

Jim Elliot (1927-1956) was a 28-year-old missionary to Ecuador who along with four other missionaries was martyred by the Waodani tribe, the very tribe he had come to preach the Gospel. He submitted to the invisible, impelled force to give his life to reach this tribe. His commitment to move forward no matter what the cost is made clear in these words that he wrote while in college: "Rest in this—it is His business to lead, command, impel, send, call or whatever you want to call it. It is your business to obey, follow, move, respond, or what have you."[24]

Valley of Elah—*Valley of Battle*

The Valley of Elah is located about sixteen miles from Hebron and is the place where David defeated Goliath. Also, located in the Valley of Elah is the Cave of Adullam where David's mighty men gathered in loyalty to David against Saul. The valley gets its name from the huge Elah tree, a type of Oak famous in that area and still present to this very day.[25]

The Valley of Elah is a place of battle—where you are confronted with the forces of Satan and the trickery of man. The battles you fight in this valley will define your future. It was in the Valley of Elah that David defeated Goliath. David's destiny was determined by the victory he secured on that day. It was the tipping point of his life.

British-born Canadian journalist, author, and pop sociologist Malcolm Gladwell (1963-) wrote a book called *The Tipping Point* where he defines the *tipping point* as "the levels at which the momentum for change become unstoppable." It is the point of critical mass, the threshold, the boiling point. Gladwell created what he calls the Three Laws of Epidemic (agents of change)—The Law of the Few, The Stickiness Factor, and The Power of Context.

The Law of the Few states that the success of any kind of social epidemic is heavily dependent on the involvement of people with a particular and rare set of social gifts.[26] David was that man. He was called and gifted for a particular task. His defeat of Goliath, Saul and the Philistines created a social epidemic. David was a messenger of change and his victories in battle lifted Israel to a place of recognition in the surrounding countries.

The Stickiness Factor affirms that the specific content of a message renders its impact memorable.[27] David's message stuck. The message that David declared to Goliath became the rallying call of all of Israel.

> *"This day will the LORD deliver thee into mine hand; and I will smite thee, and take thine head from thee; and I will give the carcases of the host of the Philistines this day unto the fowls of the air, and to the wild beasts of the earth; that all the earth may know that there is a God in Israel."*
>
> —1 SAMUEL 17:46

Jehovah is our God, and we will serve no other god. His message was refined in the place of battle and today we still speak of the victory of David over Goliath. His message is an encouragement to all who face giants in their lives.

The Power of Context contends that human behavior is sensitive to and strongly influenced by its environment.[28] The environment around David gave rise to his success in Israel. The environment was the Philistines—perennial enemy of Israel. While Goliath was chanting his diatribes against Israel, David was preparing to change the course of history. In that battle David created a tipping point, and Goliath provided that opportunity.

We all have battles. They might not be as momentous as David's but they are just as important to our success. You will have battles with yourself, with others and with the culture around you. How will you handle those battles?

Sun Tzu, traditionally thought to be the author of *The Art of War*, created principles of war that have influenced Asian and Western civilization. Tzu made it clear that the only way to handle your battles is to know your enemy. *It is said that if you know your enemies and know yourself, you will not be imperiled in a hundred battles; if you do not know your enemies but do know yourself, you will win one and lose one; if you do not know your enemies nor yourself, you will be imperiled in every single battle.*[29]

Leadership and character are defined on the field of battle. How you comport yourself in the heat of battle will distinguish you among your peers and establish you in God's purpose for your life. The battle cannot be avoided. It must be embraced with valor, tenacity and skill.

Anybody can manage things in the time of peace but it takes real men and women to succeed in the face of conflict. Victories in the private place will prepare us for triumph in the public place. Goliath was not David's first victim. Before Goliath there had been both a lion and a bear. His victory over the lion and the bear prepared him to face Goliath, and so will your skirmishes prepare you to face larger battles.

I've fought all my life. I fought battles when I was a kid growing up—malnutrition, abandonment and isolation. I started this ministry in New York City fighting for my life, my vision, and my call. Every day is a battle—people who oppose me, finances that need to be raised, lives that need to be changed, staff that needs to be guided, and dealing with my own inner struggles.

I am not here to win a popularity contest. I am here to win the battle for the souls of those who have been forsaken and forgotten. I am not looking to impress people with my gifts and ministry. I am here to reverse the curses of Satan that have been imposed upon those all around me. That is my passion. That is my purpose, and no battle will deny what I seek.

Valley of Eshcol—*Valley of Decision*

The Old Testament book of Numbers chapter 13 describes the Valley of Eshcol as a valley in the southern Negev where Israel camped right before going into the Promised Land. It was a fruitful land with huge clusters of fruit. The land was there for their taking. They had a decision to make. Shall we go in and take this land? The twelve spies were sent out from this place and came back with their report. Yes, it is a fruitful place but it is also a place of giants. Ten of the spies were distracted by the giants, but Joshua and Caleb said, "We can go in. We can take this place" (see Numbers 13:28-30).

They put it up for a vote and the ten spies vetoed the call to go into the land. What a dumb decision! You don't take a vote when God has already spoken. There is only one appropriate answer to God's Word. Yes!

Good leaders will make the right decision even if it is an unpopular one. They will not be distracted by the trivial and irrelevant. They are able to see what others cannot see.

All of us have been in that valley when we had to make a critical decision in our lives. Political correctness is ruining this country. We are afraid to make the right decision—afraid that we might offend somebody. Good leaders will make the right decision even if it is an unpopular one. There is a Chinese proverb that goes something like this, "A wise man makes his own decisions; an ignorant man follows the public opinion." This is the gap that exists between a good leader and a weak leader. A good leader does not follow the polls. He makes his decisions based upon the power of perceptions and never looks back.

If you do what you know, you will know what to do. If you know what is right, you will know what to do. The pathway to finding what is right is in learning what is important and what must be ignored. Author, physician, inventor, and consultant Edward de Bono (1933-), one of the leading authorities on creative thinking, explained that an expert is someone who has succeeded in making decisions and judgments simpler through knowing what to pay attention to and what to ignore.[30] Good leaders will not be distracted by the trivial and irrelevant. They are able to see what others cannot see.

Learning to make good decisions is a process that starts early in life. Life is about making decisions, and we learn from the decisions that we make. You make decisions based upon what you know and the more you know, the better your decisions. Sitting on the sidelines never prepared anyone for the big decisions of life. You have to get involved in life and learn from your mistakes and failures.

Good decision-makers know how to plan for the inevitable, prepare for the impossible, process the complicated, and proceed with full force when a decision is made.

In 1 Corinthians 16:8-9 Paul wrote, "But I will tarry at Ephesus until Pentecost. For a great door and effectual is opened unto me, and there are many adversaries." Open doors require decisions. What do you do when you are standing before a potential door? Paul said that there was a very important door standing before him. It was a door of opportunity, even though there were many obstacles in the way. The Greek word for *open* in the perfect tense means that "someone had opened a door for him." God opened the door. It was an open door of opportunity. When you see a door of opportunity, it becomes a door of obligation. You must go through that door. Who knows how long it will remain open? Go through the door now while it is open.

Hesitation could be disastrous. I've watched enough doors open and close in my life and I know that if you wait too long they will close. There was a theatre on Broadway and Grove that I had a chance to obtain for the ministry. We used to have a "Life Club" in that theater and it would have been a perfect place for us. I choked, and I missed it. We lost an opportunity. That's why when the opportunity came up to get our present building, I felt the obligation to get it right away. That is leadership. You learn from your mistakes.

I never said that good leaders do not make mistakes, but they learn from their mistakes. I did not choke on the decision the next time. I made a quick decision and we got the building. When the door opened to get that building, I knew we did not have the money and in the natural, we should not have pursued that direction. But this was a spiritual matter. I knew we must have it, and I knew that God was on my side.

It was a door of opportunity. It was door of obligation, but it was also a door of opposition. Great decisions always come with opposition. Just because it is the right thing to do does not mean it will be the easy thing to do. Teflon rhinos will weigh the opposition, count the cost, and then go through the door.

Valley of Achor—*Valley of Discipline*

Many identify the Valley of Achor with "the Wady Kelt, which descends through a deep ravine from the Judean hills and runs between steep banks south of the modern Jericho to Jordan, the stream after rams becoming a foaming torrent."[31]

The name *Achor* means "trouble," not so much from the geographical terrain but because of what happened there. Joshua 7 describes the Valley where Achan and his family were stoned to death because of his sin. Israel was fresh off the tremendous victory at Jericho. God put a ban on all things inside the city. What did Achan do? He took some of the booty and hid it from Israel. Ai was the next city in the path of Israel. With great confidence they attacked the city, and to their surprise, they were soundly defeated. This is the only defeat for Israel recorded in the Book of Joshua. When Achan's sin was uncovered, he was disciplined.

> Disobedience will halt your progress and set you back. Obedience will bring harmony, strengthen and empower you to continue the journey.

In memory of Achan's sin, Achor has become known as the valley of discipline where disobedience is judged. Obedience is not an option. It is critical for life in the valley. Disobedience will halt your progress and set you back. Known as "The Peace Pilgrim," American pacifist and peace activist Mildred Norman (1908-1981) explained the problem posed by disobedience in this way. "The purpose of problems is to push you toward obedience to God's laws, which are exact and cannot be changed. We have the free will to obey them or disobey them. Obedience will bring harmony; disobedience will bring you more problems."[32]

The discipline that happens in the Valley of Achor is not a bad thing. Discipline is a teacher of the wise. If we respond wisely to God's discipline, we will again see the high places. If we choose to continue in our disobedience, we will only delay our destiny.

Discipline is a refining fire in which your potential becomes ability. Everyone has potential but until it is tested, it remains only what it is—potential. Unless our muscles are exercised, they will atrophy into weakness. Discipline will strengthen us and give us power to continue the journey.

Valley of Gehenna—*Valley of Death*

The Valley of Gehenna, also known as the Valley of Hinnom was located south and west of the city of Jerusalem. It was in this valley that idolatrous Jews sacrificed their children to the god Molech (see 2 Chronicles 28:3, 33:6; Jer. 7:31, 19:2-6), where Ahaz and Manasseh made their children "pass through the fire," and it eventually became the location of the common garbage dump for Jerusalem. It then became known as the place of the dead, where dead bodies of animals and criminals were taken to be consumed by the constantly burning fires.

At some point all of us will pass through the valley of death. The older we get the more people we say goodbye to as they pass over to the other side. When we are young, we think of ourselves as immortal and too often live recklessly because of that thought.

Death is a reality but the good point is the promise that He will walk with us through this valley toward a better life on the other side. There is no reason to fear as we get ready to pass through that valley.

Death puts things into perspective. It makes frivolous the little hassles that we go through in this life. When you are staring at eternity, you aren't concerned about the superficial things of this life. To prepare to enter the Valley of Death one must live this life fully accomplishing everything he was intended to. Once he has done that he will be ready to cross over to his reward.

On the eve of his passing over, the apostle Paul confirmed this truth in his words to Timothy.

> *I have fought the good fight, I have finished my course, I have kept the faith: Henceforth there is laid up for me a crown of righteousness, which the Lord, the righteous judge, shall give me at that day: and not to me only, but unto all them also that love his appearing.*
>
> —2 TIMOTHY 4:7-8

Life is full of valleys and the test we must pass is to survive in the valley. The only way to endure is to understand that you are not alone. God has promised that He will walk with us through even the darkest valley. You are never alone. The final rewards will be given to those who have passed the test, have successfully passed through the last valley and reached the distant shore. And when we reach that final place, the only words we want to hear are: "Well done, good and faithful servant. Enter into the joy of your Lord" (Matthew 25:23).

Chapter 8

HASSLE IN YOUR HARVEST

No one is so brave that he is not disturbed by something unexpected.[33]

THE ONLY THING IN life that is predictable is that life is unpredictable. No one cruises down the highway of life without facing detours caused by the unexpected. There is no way that you can effectively plan your life and eliminate the startling intrusion of the unforeseen. You cannot calculate your future. My philosophy of life is: *expect the unexpected.* It is an inevitable truth of living in this world. Even the most polished GPS system cannot help you to avoid the diversions that are just around the corner.

A teflon rhino knows how to navigate through the unexpected even if the unanticipated things of life have been caused by his own doing. The ability to deal with the unexpected is what separates the strong from the weak. How does one react when unwanted weeds attack the seeds he has sown? The classic story of the Sower and the Seed as told by Jesus provides clues on dealing with the unexpected.

> *Another parable put he forth unto them, saying, The kingdom of heaven is likened unto a man which sowed good seed in his field: But while men slept, his enemy came and sowed tares among the wheat, and went his way. But when the blade was*

sprung up, and brought forth fruit, then appeared the tares also. So the servants of the householder came and said unto him, Sir, didst not thou sow good seed in thy field? From whence then hath it tares? Or why are there tares? It looked like and boy, this is good. It looked like you sowed good seed, so where did the tares come from? He said unto them, An enemy hath done this. The servants said unto him, Wilt thou then that we go and gather them up? But he said, Nay; lest while ye gather up the tares, ye root up also the wheat with them. Let both grow together until the harvest: and in the time of harvest I will say to the reapers, Gather ye together first the tares, and bind them in bundles to burn them: but gather the wheat into my barn.

—Matthew 13:24-30

Hassle in Your Harvest

There is a process of progression in every life when something comes at you unexpectedly. Life does throw curves. It is inevitable. Not every morning will greet you with the warmth and beauty of the sun. There will be rainy, gloomy days. Your success in life depends on how you manage the unanticipated surprises that bounce into it.

Most of us do well when we see a storm forming on the horizon, and we can adjust our plans for the day. If we know that it is possible that we might lose our job, then we can engage in a search for alternative employment. But when we are called into our employer's office unexpectedly and the horrifying message is delivered that we are fired, what do we do?

Jesus tells the story of a certain man who plants *good* seed in his field. The field is a good field. The seed is good seed. During the night something terrible happens. Someone plants *tares* in the field. A *tare* is a "darnel, a species of harmful grass that looks like wheat, but is not wheat."

The tare *appeared* out of nowhere. Unaware that his field has been sabotaged by an enemy, the farmer is uncertain what to do. He has lethal tares growing right alongside of his good wheat. If he attempts to pull up the tares, he runs the almost inevitable risk of damaging his wheat crop. He is facing an agricultural conundrum.

There is a kingdom principle hidden in this story—a story of supreme significance that few people seem to grasp in its concealed consequences. *If you want to change what you're reaping, then you have to change what you're sowing.* We keep praying that God will change our situation and deliver us from our problems. But while we are praying this prayer, we keep engaging in the same destructive patterns. If you want better results you have to change what you are doing. I believe it was the German-born Swiss-American theoretical physicist, philosopher and author, Albert Einstein (1879-1955) who is credited with saying that the definition of insanity is doing the same thing over and over and expecting different results.

If you desire a different harvest in your life, you have to do something different in your life. You need to sow different seed in the soil of your life. When a person gets saved, they often think that everything is going to be all right. This is the promise the preacher has made to them. What the preacher forgot to tell them is that even though we are now saved, we still face the possibility of reaping things that we did in our previous life. Sometimes it takes time to sort through—to get rid of the bad seed that you have sowed in the past. You must not get discouraged in the process of dealing with some of the residual fallout of a previous life.

In Galatians 6:7 the apostle Paul pens a powerful aphorism, "Whatsoever a man soweth, that shall he also reap." One act of bad sowing can destroy a whole field. Something *appears* in our life and we wonder where it came from, forgetting that bad seed we planted sometime back. Lust if not dealt with can destroy a life, a ministry.

How often I have watched this destructive pattern in the lives of God's leaders!

We pray for a tree in our life, and God gives us an acorn. What we don't understand is that life is about *process.* It takes time to get the tree. We are an impatient society. I have watched what I have come to call the "McDonaldization" of our culture and its contemptible consequences. Fast food leads to fat living. Fast cash leads to fraudulent lifestyles. Anything that comes to us without effort will not be appreciated and will not be preserved.

> *In those days there was no king in Israel: every man did that which was right in his own eyes.*
>
> —JUDGES 21:25

The issue is not that people did the wrong thing. The issue is that they did what was right in their own eyes. They followed the path created by their own imagination of what was correct and appropriate. This sums up the culture of our day. There is no absolute truth any longer. Truth is in the eye of the beholder. When we deny the existence of the King, we make ourselves kings. We reject absolute truth. The result is that truth becomes existential based upon every person's own experience. The do-your-own-thing philosophy that emerged out of the hippie culture of the 60s and 70s planted a bad seed of individualism and self-determinism. This self-inflicted virus has created a field full of tares.

The Inevitability of the Tares

"There was a tare planted among the wheat." Life cannot be lived without tares. They are inevitable. No matter how hard you try, you cannot prevent the presence of bad seed cropping up. Sometimes it is your fault, but sometimes it is the work of others sent to discourage and destroy you. I have had to face my own series of tares in my life. I had to face the issue of abandonment when my own mother left me on a street corner. I have had to bear the pain of being shot. I didn't expect these things to happen. They came suddenly, without warning.

Someone once said that with new levels come new devils. I have found that to be true. The greater the cause, the greater the opposition! Inevitably, the will of God collides with the schemes of the enemy. New assignments are always accompanied by new adversity.

> Those on the front lines are the easiest target and can be picked off by the devil's sharp shooters. They predict the unpredictable and prepare for the inescapable.

Tares are designed to discourage you, to knock you off track, to rattle and disillusion you. Twelve hundred ministers a month are quitting the ministry—walking away with their heads hanging. How can this be? They were not prepared for the inevitability of the tares. They became disillusioned by failure, discouraged by opposition, and distracted by pain.

They should have been aware that no good thing comes without effort and heartache. People have stolen money from us, thrown me off of buildings, pushed me in front of trains, stabbed and shot me in an effort to discourage me. But I understand that there is a price to be paid if you are a leader. Those on the front lines are the easiest target and can be picked off by the devil's sharp shooters.

Successful leadership expects the unexpected. They are aware of the crouching tiger that seeks to prevent their progress. They are not afraid of the unexplained and the unforeseen. They predict the unpredictable and prepare for the inescapable.

It seems that every project costs more than they said and every task takes longer than predicted. But a wise leader is not shocked or discouraged.

There is another side to the inevitability of the tares. Too many of our tares were planted by us. In my experience, you know exactly where ninety-five percent of the problems you have in your life came from. They didn't just pop up. It is the law of sowing and reaping. Some tares are planted by others, but we plant a lot of them ourselves. And we should not be surprised by the tares that arise, the tares we have planted. Don't blame the devil for all your problems. In many cases, you sowed it, so you reaped it.

A girl I was dealing with back in New York came to me and said, "I'm pregnant." And then she said, "I can't believe this happened." I was stunned. How stupid could this girl be? I am convinced that there wasn't some demon that was sitting on top of her bed making her commit this sexual act that led to the pregnancy.

You wonder why checks bounce? It is not the devil's fault. He gets blamed for a lot of things that we do. Your careless spending led to that bounced check. You cannot expect to balance your budget if you are spending faster than you are depositing.

God Allows Things to Happen

Sometimes the enemy plants seeds in your garden. Sometimes you plant the tares. But there are times when God allows it to happen. That is not a popular theology. Sometimes God has to harden Pharaoh's heart to get His people to the Promised Land. There are times when God allows things to happen in order to get you to the place He promised. No one ever said it would be easy. If they did, they were lying.

There are moments in our lives when God must apply force in order to create a reaction that will guide us to the place where we were meant to be.

Every so often God has to allow things to happen in your life. Bad things can happen to good people. At times the only way God can get our attention is to introduce a little adversity. In physics, motion means a change in location as the result of an *applied force.* Sir Isaac Newton (1643-1727), English physicist, mathematician, astronomer, and theologian, in what has become known as Newton's Third Law of Motion, states that for every action there is an equal and opposite reaction.

There are moments in our lives when God must *apply* force in order to create a reaction that will guide us to the place we were meant to be. John McDonald put it this way, "There must be a positive and negative in everything in the universe in order to complete a circuit or circle, without which there would be no activity, no motion" [34]

The Holy Spirit is an applied force. You have to ask yourself this question, "What does it take for the Spirit of God to move me?" What does it take for Him to get your attention? Sometimes it only takes the "still, small voice" mentioned in 1 Kings 19:12. Other times it takes a ball bat on top of your head. There are times when God must *arrest* you with a divinely designed situation in order to halt your wayward ways.

Not only does God use adversity to get our attention, He also uses it to strengthen our character and expand our vision. God will often allow things to happen to let you see some things that you are probably just not going to notice under normal conditions. The "toughness" that is massaged into the fabric of our being by difficult times prepares us for our future. Without that character we could not sustain what God wants to do through us.

The Fix is Worse than the Problem

What did the master's servants say when they saw the problem in the field? "Do you want us to go in and pull up the tares?" Most humans have an innate compulsion to fix things. I have to admit that it is more of a guy thing. Guys like to fix things and girls like to talk about things. Don't accuse me of being overly simplistic for there is truth in that statement.

In our drive toward self-preservation, we create cures that are worse than the sickness. The self-absorption that occurs as we seek to correct our image, cure our pain and change our lives only serves to create worse problems. Be careful of quick fixes.

The law of unintended consequences states that the actions of people always have effects that are unanticipated or unintended. I'll give you an example. Let's say that you are facing a critical financial problem, and out of fear, you take out a huge loan that you know you are not capable of handling. Unintentionally you have just made your problem worse. The cure becomes worse than the illness.

History has taught us that human beings are notoriously bad at rectifying problems. Every solution brings with it another problem that must be solved. But we are never willing to admit that we cannot fix the problem, and fear often drives us to jump in and do something even if that something has catastrophic implications. We trump our fear with our pride.

It is our pride that drives us to pull up the tares. We think we have the ability to fix any situation. Pride is at the bottom of all mistakes. There are times when ignorance gets us into trouble, but it is pride that keeps us there. There is a certain pride that will not allow us to admit we do not know what to do. We must rise above this fear and with humility admit that we cannot fix the problem.

Leave it Alone

In Matthew 13, Jesus said the master told his servants to leave the field alone when they asked if they should pull out the tares. He instructed them to do nothing! That sounds crazy. Surely we have to do something. No! Jesus said to leave it alone. Be patient. We have to be patient and wait on God for the solution. There is a Dutch proverb that tells us a handful of patience is worth more than a bushel of brains.

> *But they that wait upon the LORD shall renew their strength; they shall mount up with wings as eagles; they shall run, and not be weary; and they shall walk, and not faint.*
> —Isaiah 40:31

In the face of problems there is power in patience. Between the question and the answer there is the waiting. Sometimes all we can do is to wait for heaven to answer. Don't call. Don't write. Don't try to straighten it out. Don't react. Don't flip out. Don't freak out. Wait on the Lord!

You have to learn that sometimes you can't fix your problems, much less the problems of others. Some preachers think they are the *Answer Man,* "You got a problem? Come to me. I have your answer." Life just doesn't work that way. There are times when there are no answers. There are times when all we need is a shoulder to lean on—not an answer blurted out from the mouths of the righteous.

Waiting is tough. It goes against our natural instincts. Occasionally there will be times when all you *should* do, when all you *can* do is wait. John Quincy Adams (1767-1848), sixth President of the United States said that patience and perseverance have a magical effect before which difficulties disappear and obstacles vanish.[35] From time to time an answer will appear as we wait. We might not see it initially, but as we linger we begin to see the emergence of a solution.

Timing is Everything

Jesus gives the appropriate answer to this troubling situation. "When the time is right…. Let it go, and when the time is right, we will deal with the problem of the tares. Don't go in there and try to rip everything apart. Let it go for now." And when the time is right He said, "I'll handle it." I hope you can get this powerful principle. If you choose to accept the timing of the Lord, you will succeed in life. If not, you will be doomed to failure.

When the unexpected impinges on the edges of your life, realize that there is a purpose in the pain.

Solomon said in Ecclesiastes 3:1, "To every thing there is a season, and a *time* to every purpose under the heaven." If you try to reap in the wrong season, you will not reap what you sowed. You will only destroy your harvest. Moses was chosen by God to be a champion for Israel, but he nearly ruined his destiny when he killed the Egyptian.

Why does God want us to wait? He's trying to get us to see something. He is trying to get us somewhere. The hassle in your harvest is there for a reason. When the unexpected impinges on the edges of your life, realize that there is a purpose in the pain. Then you must realize that timing is the key to the resolution of the hassle in the harvest. If you leave the timing to God, you will enjoy the final victory. Trust His timing!

Stacey Charter is not a famous person, but she is a survivor. She survived cancer, a divorce, and other attacks on her life. Her quotes on life are all over the Internet. She has a great philosophy of life. Concerning timing, she says: "Life is all about timing…the unreachable becomes reachable, the unavailable become available, the unattainable...attainable. Have the patience, wait it out. It's all about timing."[36]

Hassles in your harvest seek to distract you, to destroy you, to discredit you, and to disillusion you. There have been people in my life who have sought to discredit me. I have had others rip me off for millions of dollars. However, I have made a decision that I will not seek my own revenge. I will not defend myself. I will allow God's timing to deliver me from those seeking to harm me and He has come through every time!

Trouble always precedes victory. Maybe you're about to lose your house. Maybe you're about to lose your wife. Maybe you've already lost your kids. And maybe your life is just falling apart. I understand that. I understand that more than you know. But let me just say this. Let God do what He wants to do in your life. He's trying to make something of your life. If you let Him, He will resolve the hassle in your harvest!

Chapter 9

THE THEOLOGY OF
THE THRESHING

Life is a process of becoming, a combination of states we have to go through. Where people fail is that they wish to elect a state and remain in it. This is a kind of death."[37]

INSTANT SUCCESS IS DECEPTIVE. It tricks you into thinking that achievement comes without cost and persistence. Life is a process. In order to get from where you are to where you need to go will not happen without preparation, planning, and process. Purpose cannot be achieved without process, but process must always be understood in the context of purpose. We must understand where we are going and that we cannot get there quickly.

It is more important to know where you are going than to get there quickly. Do not mistake activity for achievement.[38]

During the process vision is honed, purpose is refined, and character is developed. The key is not to get lost in the process and lose sight of the purpose. If we don't comprehend the purpose of the process, we run the danger of getting lost, cynical and discouraged before we reach our ultimate goal.

Some people respond to the process very well. Some people learn from the process. Some people grow by the process. But if you've been around for a while you'll notice a lot of people do not.

There are those who just don't get it. They misinterpret God's hand in the process and this mistake in judgment can lead to self-pity, guilt and anger.

A part of the process is preparation. God is preparing us to go to a place we have never been before. But we cannot survive in that place without preparation and adjustment. There are times that we get off track and need a course adjustment. As we have already stated there are times when that adjustment comes with a Divine applied force that gets us moving in the right direction.

In Isaiah 28 we discover some critical keys to insightful awareness of the purpose of the process. God is speaking prophetically through an agricultural illustration. He is not simply giving a lesson on how to prepare the seed for proper planting in the field. Accurate biblical interpretation requires work to understand the principle that lies hidden in the presentation of these basic tips of good farming.

Purpose of the Threshing

Give ye ear, and hear my voice; hearken, and hear my speech. Doth the plowman plow all day to sow? doth he open and break the clods of his ground? When he hath made plain the face thereof, doth he not cast abroad the fitches, and scatter the cummin, and cast in the principal wheat and the appointed barley and the rie in their place? For his God doth instruct him to discretion, and doth teach him. For the fitches are not threshed with a threshing instrument, neither is a cart wheel turned about upon the cummin; but the fitches are beaten out with a staff, and the cummin with a rod. Bread corn is bruised; because he will not ever be threshing it, nor break it with the wheel of his cart, nor bruise it with his horsemen.

—Isaiah 28:23-28

God is talking to His people. When God talks, people should listen! In this discourse God is telling Israel that they had better get ready, because some hard times were on the way. He gave no indication what the hard times would be or why they were coming. We do know that God's ultimate purpose was to get them to a new and better place.

The threshing floor was a place where the seed was separated from the chaff, the pure from the impure, the original from the replica, and the seed from the weed.

> We are wrong if we think every problem that comes into our lives is because we have sinned.

We know that the threshing has a purpose. God is not an ogre who simply delights in punishing people. God is a good God, and when trouble interrupts our comfortable existence, that trouble comes with Divine purpose.

I have survived more than thirty years of ministry because I've learned that there is a purpose in the threshing. I have not given up in the battle because I know that the ultimate victory is there waiting for me.

The threshing process has several purposes. It is not always the result of sin. We are wrong if we think every problem that comes into our lives is because we have sinned. *God's trying to smack me. It's a punishing thing.* No! Most challenging situations that come into our lives have a higher purpose than punishment. God knows that the only way to get us to the place Divinely designed for us is to travel down the path of pain. That pathway has a purpose and we must never lose sight of it.

The Seed and the Threshing

God talks about three different kinds of seeds in these verses from Isaiah—fitches, cumin and corn. All three are different, and they are processed differently with unique purposes in mind. In the threshing process the seed was thrown on the floor and a tool was used to beat out the chaff. It is a prepping process. The purpose is to separate the seed. The seed is the gold.

Fitch is a spice, an herb of sweet savor. The ancient people used the fitch seed in bread to give it a more agreeable taste and *fragrance*. Have you ever gone by a bakery when they are baking bread? The aroma drifting out of that bakery is irresistible. Even if you're not hungry, you're hungry when that scent reaches your nostrils. It's that aroma, that fragrance that comes from a type of fitch that is added to the yeast and creates a unique fragrance.

Cumin is a member of the parsley family and grows to the height of one or two feet. It is similar to a caraway seed. Cumin is the second most popular spice, second only to pepper. It is a popular *flavor* often used in Mexican and Indian food. It was a common spice used in biblical times.

Corn of the Bible is not the corn we know. A better translation would be grain and would include both barley and wheat. Corn was a primary *food* of ancient times. It was symbolic of abundance and wealth.

The threshing process of the fitch, cumin, and corn has significant differences. The fitch is reaped before the threshing process and is very delicate. You don't have to smack it hard in order to break the seed. Cumin is not as delicate, but still more delicate than the corn. All three have to be threshed, but there is a different threshing process for each type of seed.

The fitch is known for its fragrance. The cumin is known for its flavor, and the corn is known as food. The fragrance of a product is not as important as its flavor. The flavor is not as important as its food value. All three are important, but they have different levels of importance and serve for different values and different purposes.

Just as the seeds are uniquely different, so is the process of threshing. The fitch, being a delicate seed is threshed with a staff. The Hebrew word for *staff* is *mattah*. The word for *rod* and *staff* are sometimes the same Hebrew word. In this case, they are different words and do not mean the same thing. In this passage, the staff is a stick. The stick is held in the hand of the farmer and is lifted up and down pounding out the fitch. You do not have to use a lot of force and effort to split that seed because as we said it is very delicate.

The cumin is beaten with a rod. The Hebrew word for *rod* is *shabat.* Many times the rod that was used for threshing would be pointed. The cumin is a little tougher and has to be threshed with a pointed rod in order to break open the seed.

The corn is the hardest of the seeds and requires a threshing machine in order to prepare for its purpose. The threshing machine is more like a grinding wheel or sometimes a threshing wheel drawn over the grain. The threshing instrument is uniquely designed for the seed.

Now we move to the spiritual significance of this information. When your life enters into a threshing process, it has a specific course of action. God does not thresh you to destroy you. He threshes you for the purpose of preparation. You will suffer in this life. That should not come to you as some surprise. In Romans 8:17, Paul explained to the church at Rome that suffering is a process that leads us into the place of glory: "And if children, then heirs; heirs of God, and joint-heirs with Christ; if so be that we suffer with him, that we may be also glorified together."

You cannot get to the place of glory except by the way of suffering. Suffering is a process that has a purpose. The suffering of this life will produce fragrance, flavor, and food in your life. The threshing comes with different intensity according to the purpose.

"You are the salt of the earth; but if the salt loses its flavor, how shall it be seasoned? It is then good for nothing but to be thrown out and trampled underfoot by men" (Matthew 5:13, NKJV). There is a process of threshing that creates a certain flavor. The flavor enhances the taste of the food. Part of the attraction of the food is its flavor. The purpose of the process is to enable us to have a certain flavor in our lives that will attract others. If that flavor is lost by sin, neglect, and time then it has lost its value. There is great value in the flavor of your life that is developed through the process of preparation.

> People were attracted to Jesus because of the authority in His words and the power of His acts.

"For we are to God the fragrance of Christ among those who are being saved and among those who are perishing" (2 Corinthians 2:15, NASV). Fragrance also has a similar purpose—the purpose of attraction. Your words and actions have a certain attraction value to them. People were attracted to Jesus because of the authority in His words and the power of His acts. Authority and power are developed in the processes of life. They are not learned in a seminary or Bible college.

"These people are like land that gets plenty of rain. A farmer plants and cares for the land so that it will produce food. If it grows plants that help people, then it has God's blessing" (Hebrews 6:7, Easy to Read Version). The ultimate goal of fragrance and flavor is to attract people to the food. What spiritual food do you have to offer to others? Fine foods are produced and processed in the kitchen of life.

One of the dangers we face in life is when we become focused on the process and not the purpose. When the battles confront us, when the struggles overcome us, and when the issues confuse us, we get lost in the process. Victimization and self-absorption takes over. *Nobody loves me. Everybody hates me. No one cares about what I am going through. No one understands the trouble I see.* Don't yield to the seductive pull of self-pity. Acting like a victim threatens your future.

Did you ever wonder why Paul said in 2 Corinthians 12:7, "I have a thorn in the flesh"? I thought it was interesting that he used the word "thorn." A thorn is an irritation that distracts us from the moment we are living in. Paul came to realize that the thorn was part of the process of maintaining his humility. There is a purpose to the thorn, and those who either misunderstand or reject the thorn will remain in their pride and immaturity.

We must understand that the process leads to purpose and that knowledge will give us hope and courage in order to endure. "And not only [so], but we also boast in the tribulations, knowing that the tribulation doth work endurance; and the endurance, experience; and the experience, hope" (Romans 5:3-4, Young's Literal New Testament).

Endurance is the key to surviving the process. Paul sets out the process in this verse, showing that as we embrace the trouble, it will create experiences that deepen our character. Character will strengthen our hope in the final outcome for our lives. This is the process that leads to the purpose.

Observations on the Threshing Process

The first observation I have noticed in life is that the threshing process doesn't crush, it *separates*. It doesn't crush. It separates. If it was crushed, then it could not be used. If the seed is not threshed properly, the seed will be destroyed. Certain seeds are sensitive and do not need a heavy threshing. Perhaps you are delicate. You don't need much prodding to get the message. You are among the fragrance people who have tender spirits. You are tender to the things of God. The fragrance people are very open and receptive. It doesn't take much for God to get their attention. A little "bop" and they are all ears, repentant and obedient.

> God is transforming us to be His agents of change in a world gone awry.

The separation removes the outer core so that the inner seed can be revealed. The outer man is dealt with so that the inner man can be manifested. In every man there are two men. There is an outer man who is the person that all of us see. But there is an inner man who no one sees. The outer man may be persecuted, betrayed, hurt, wounded and even killed. But the inner man is not harmed by what it suffers in its body. In fact, the inner man is empowered and enlarged by what it goes through in its outer shell. Paul puts it this way: "For which cause we faint not; but though our outward man perish, yet the inward man is renewed day by day" (2 Corinthians 4:16).

The second observation is that the threshing *prepares*. It doesn't destroy, it prepares. It prepares the seed to be made into food. It prepares it for transformation. *Personal transformation can and does have global effects. As we go, so goes the world, for the world is us. The revolution that will save the world is ultimately a personal one.*[39] God is preparing us, transforming us to be His agents of change in a world gone awry.

The important thing to note at this point is that the threshing does not last forever. God knows what you need and will not go beyond what you are able to handle. There is a set or prescribed timing to all things in God. "For his anger endureth but a moment; in his favour is life: weeping may endure for a night, but joy cometh in the morning" (Psalms 30:5).

How long is the moment? No one knows. The only thing we know is that it is not forever. It would counter God's purpose to endure perpetual threshing. God's mercy intervenes once the preparation is complete.

The final thing to note is that the process is determined by the *purpose.* For years I never understood why I went through the things I went through at such a young age. There was so much rejection, so many battles, and so much heartache. Now I understand. The pain came with purpose. I had a destiny, and in order to attain that destiny, I had to go through the process that separated and prepared me for my future. Eventually the preparation opens the door for the purpose to be revealed. I was being sharpened to live on the cutting edge.

Now I know. Now I understand. I endured all of that opposition to prepare me for my purpose. Now I am fighting bigger demons as I have advanced to the next level. The little responsibility that I had when I was younger prepared me to handle a heavier burden. When you are going through the process, you don't understand.

There were many times when I said that I did not sign up for this. But I kept forging ahead. I did the only thing I could do. I *presented* myself to God. I said the only thing that I could say, "Here am I." I learned faithfulness and faithfulness brought me to a place of greater levels of ministry.

Maybe you can't sing or play a guitar or preach from a platform. But God is preparing you for something. You have your own unique destiny and all you have to do is find that place. That's what I did when I was nineteen. They said, "We need somebody to drive the van to pick up these kids." That was my first summer out of Bible school.

I said, "Yeah, I can do it." Did I think when I volunteered to drive the Volkswagen van that day that it would lead to a worldwide ministry? No! I was just faithful at the moment and that is all that God asks. He is not asking for great things. He is asking for faithfulness in the small things. That faithfulness will lead to the big things.

Not everybody can be the flavoring. Not everyone can be the fragrance. Everybody can't be the food. But everybody can present themselves to the Lord and say, "Lord, whatever place You want me to be, whatever spot You want me to fill, how You want to use me, I will be faithful. I will give myself to You."

Beware of the shortcuts. There is no shortcut that will eliminate the process that leads to your purpose. Shortcuts only get you into trouble and delay the process. Sometimes you get tired. Sometimes you just don't want to go any further. Sometimes you don't like the pain. I don't like the pain either. I don't like a lot of the things I've gone through. But I clearly understand that there are no shortcuts to the process.

Do you want to be used of God? Better think about it. Do you want to make a difference? Do you want to serve God in your generation? Before you answer these questions, please be sure that you are willing to go through the threshing. For every great man or woman of God, there is a history of persecution, pain, rejection, disappointment, and heartache. They did not discover the theology of the threshing in a classroom, but on the field of life.

Be ready to embrace the process, endure the agony as you present yourself to God as a living sacrifice. Your sacrifice will release the fragrance of Christ, reveal the flavor of the Gospel, and you will become food for the hungry and desperate people around you.

Chapter 10

WOUNDED WARRIORS

To be a warrior is not a simple matter of wishing to be one. It is rather an endless struggle that will go on to the very last moment of our lives. Nobody is born a warrior, in exactly the same way that nobody is born an average man. We make ourselves into one or the other.[40]

WHERE THERE IS A will, there is a way. Determination and persistence are the companions of every great leader. Those that have succeeded in life are part of the company that refute the argument of those that say it can't be done and resist the attraction of those that would want to quit. They do not sit on the sidelines wishing something would happen. They are on the field of life making their dreams come true.

All soldiers in the army of God will get wounded. But the wounded warrior does not focus his attention on the pain that comes from rejection, abuse, failure or tragedy. Rather than being weakened by the opposition of others, they are reinforced by their resolve to complete the mission. Churchill once said that *success is not final, failure is not fatal: it is the courage to continue that counts.* It is our choices in the dark places that will determine our ultimate victory.

Too many people are lost on the field of battle. They hit one battle—one struggle—and that proverbial straw breaks the camel's back. There will be times in your life when it appears that everything is against you. It is one bump in the road after another. Your breath is totally sucked out of you and finally you reach the point where you cannot bounce back. A while back I was talking with a pastor who had decided to hang it up. His exact words were, "I just can't go on. I am not able to bounce back from this last situation."

The sad thing is that it is very possible that the last resistance in the middle of the battle could be the eventual moment of victory. Harriet Beecher Stowe (1811-1896), a champion in the battle against slavery and author of *Uncle Tom's Cabin,* put it this way. *"When you get into a tight place and everything goes against you, till it seems as though you could not hold on a minute longer, never give up then, for that is just the place and time that the tide will turn."*[41]

Sharp-Shooting Lefties

In Judges 20 there is an interesting story about a company of Benjaminite warriors, men that could sling a stone, left-handed, with unbelievable accuracy.

> But the children of Benjamin gathered themselves together out of the cities unto Gibeah, to go out to battle against the children of Israel. And the children of Benjamin were numbered at that time out of the cities twenty and six thousand men that drew sword, beside the inhabitants of Gibeah, which were numbered seven hundred chosen men. Among all this people there were seven hundred chosen men lefthanded; every one could sling stones at an hair breadth, and not miss.
> —JUDGES 20:14-16

In the tribe of Benjamin there were 26,000 skilled warriors. Among that number were 700 left-handed men that were powerfully accurate with the sling. These slings were not like the common slingshot we use today.

This sling was composed of a pocket made of either cloth or leather and a cord going from each side. The longer the sling was, the greater its range. Long-range slings were about three feet long. The stone was put in the piece of cloth attached to the two cords held and then whirled around the head. Then one cord was released at the right moment and the stone sped to its target at deadly speeds. There were different methods to the slinging process. Some say they were slung overhead but others insist that the more accurate method was an underhand motion.[42]

The issue that they were left-handed is an interesting one. One commentary says, "They were left handed, because they were not right handed." Well that is really ingenious, but something doesn't seem right about that description. I have spent a lot of time studying why they used their left hand, believing that there is a spiritual significance to these left-handed warriors.

The end of my quest for an answer brought me to a remarkable little village in Wales. It is Hay-on-Wye, a town of books, situated on the east bank of the River Wye. There are about thirty major bookshops in the city specializing in second hand, classic books. I love going to this little village searching for books to add to my library.

I remember one time that I was there, I eventually meandered into a shop and ended up in the basement exploring through the variety of books that were staring at me from the huge racks in front of me. I found one book that looked intriguing and pulled it out. As I browsed through the book I came across a reference to these Benjamite warriors.

The commentary gives an interesting twist to the reason why these warriors used their left hand. The author said that these 700 were at one time right-handed. At some point in a battle, they were wounded and each lost the use of his right hand. They were wounded warriors that could only use their left hand. That rang a bell with me so to speak and I believe that he had arrived at exactly the right conclusion about these Benjamites.

They were warriors who had a decision to make. They could give up and go home or make the best of their circumstances. As warriors they would not consent to going home. They made a choice. They would not leave the battlefield. That was their destiny—their chosen place of honor. They would not allow their physical disability to deter them. What did they do?

The left hand was not natural for them. If you are a right-handed person, have you ever tried to throw a ball or write with your left hand? It is not natural. It feels awkward and you don't have the same accuracy or strength. But these warriors had no choice—use the left hand or give up—so they made the best of their circumstances. Every day they practiced using their left hand until they became proficient with the left hand. They became so skilled with their left hands that they could hit their targets with regular accuracy.

Their circumstances demanded choices. Their choices were founded in their determination, and their determination led them to an alternative option. Those options kept them in the place of their destiny—on the battlefield.

When I got shot in the face there were those who thought I would give up and retire. What those people don't understand is that I can't give up. Retire and go where? Where do people like me go to retire? To Florida? To play shuffleboard? That is not a worthy option for a wounded warrior. I would rather die than retire. I know that I am chosen for a purpose, and I will not allow a little gunshot wound to force me into early retirement. I am driven by the opportunities that still exist to change the lives of those around me.

Warriors Get Wounded

Maybe you are still right handed and have never been wounded on the battlefield of life. You should be thankful that you have not had to face what others have. Let me give you some advice. Your time will come. Every warrior in the army of God will have his time. Those who choose to live their lives on the front lines will get hurt at some point. It is an inevitability of life.

I wouldn't rejoice in an easy life. The easy way is the weak way. It means that you have chosen to be at the back of the line and avoid the challenges confronting those who seek the frontlines. Choosing the place of safety and security might help you avoid pain, but it will hinder you from making the most important decisions of your life.

Strength and courage are not gifts. They are character traits that have been developed in the heat of the battle. Unless your character is tested, how do you know what your character is? The power of your character and courage is revealed on the battlefield.

The critics are those who have never been in the battle and find it easy to cast verbal barbs at those who have been wounded. They will never know what it means to have a scar. Scars are a testimony of those who have risked everything to follow Christ. The wounded way is the way of Christ. He was wounded for our transgressions. We are made whole through His pain and sacrifice. And He calls us to follow Him along the same path of pain.

It is easy to look at successful people and be envious of their accomplishments, but we do not know what has happened in their lives to get them to that arena of achievement. It's like eating at your favorite restaurant. You just love the food. You love the ambience. The service is great. If you don't want to spoil that experience, never go back into the kitchen. You don't want to know what all goes on to prepare that food.

If you can't stand the heat, get out of the kitchen. People are making huge sacrifices to make your life enjoyable. No one knows the sacrifices that others have made to make your life easier and better. In this country we are riding on the backs of those men and women in the military who are fighting on our behalf to ensure that we will continue to enjoy our freedom. They return home proudly bearing their scars—many being reduced to live the rest of their lives in wheelchairs or with artificial limbs.

 I have discovered that trouble creates a capacity to handle it.

No one knows the trouble I've seen. No one knows, but Jesus. I know that there are people out there who wish they could have a successful ministry like we have here in New York. I say, "Be careful what you wish for." You cannot give birth to a baby without the pressure of pain. No good thing comes without a great deal of failure, hurt and rejection.

I have discovered that trouble creates a capacity to handle it. No great hero is born in a classroom. They are formed in the skirmishes of life.

Here is a point that cannot be avoided. Sometimes the wounds are self-inflicted. There are times when we get backed into a corner because of our own doing. Don't blame God, the devil, or others when you are the source of your scuffles. You cannot blame the mirror if you do not look good. The only cure for self-inflicted pain is repentance, not blame. You can easily crawl out of the hole you have dug if you recognize your own wrong.

Country singer Tim McGraw released a song a few years back called "Live Like You Were Dying." In the song he talks about meeting a man whose doctors had just told him he was dying. He asked the guy, "What did you do when you got the news?" The dying man's response was terrific! He said, "I went sky diving. I went Rocky mountain climbing! I went 2.7 seconds on a bull named Fu Manchu! I loved deeper and I spoke sweeter, and I gave forgiveness I'd been denying." This is great advice. We must learn to live life like we are dying.

When your pain demands an answer, do not retreat! In that fifteen-minute drive to the emergency room after I was shot, I had a lot to think about. What do you do? That experience only served to increase my determination and resolve. Wounded warriors are not quitters and their wounds only make them stronger.

Your wounds might be physical but they can also be mental and emotional. The important thing is that what does not kill you can only strengthen you. Wounds in the midst of battle will happen. You will get hurt. The question is: What will you do with your pain?

What Will You Choose?

When you get wounded you will have two choices—give up or move on. That's it. All of your possible decisions boil down to these two choices. Will you abandon the battle or will you advance toward the enemy?

You can submit to all the counseling in the world and read all the books you want to read about the things that have caused your heartache. But in the end it is a simple decision. Will you allow your misery to lead you into resentment and retreat or will you permit your anguish to be transformed into strength and worship?

Concerning his mission in life, Martin Luther King said that "no plans had been written for retreat." The wounded warrior allows his wounds to be like the sound of a bugle in his ear, waking him up and calling him to move forward into the battle.

I've been working in this ministry for more than thirty years. I have been in the hospital too many times watching young children dying. I watched people being murdered on our streets. I have picked up little girls on our bus who have AIDS because of their drug-addicted, promiscuous mothers. It wears me out at times, but I cannot give up. I must be available and willing to save those who are still alive.

I've wondered how these things could happen. I have been stunned by the apathy of those who sit on the sidelines without any care for those who are disenfranchised by poverty, abuse, and rejection. What do I do? Can I give up? The answer is, "No." I cannot give up. While I still have life, I must fight this battle on the behalf of these precious ones. We all have our reasons for wanting to give up, but the wounded warrior will not retreat in the day of battle. There is an enemy to be defeated. There are people to be liberated. There is a battle to be won.

> Either lead or be led. The choice is yours.

Our choices define us and reveal who we really are. Life is the sum of the choices that you and I have made. Those choices bring consequences for either good or for evil. Good fortune is not created by chance, but by choices. The things we choose determine the opportunities that present themselves to us. You choose to be who you are and no one forces that upon you. You either lead or you will be led.

I don't want to waste my experiences on self-pity and regret. I want to learn from my experiences. I want to grow from my circumstances. I want to be strengthened in my battles. You can either wallow in the circumstances as they exist or decide to change your situation.

You are the person who has to decide.
Whether you'll do it or toss it aside;
You are the person who makes up your mind.
Whether you'll lead or will linger behind.
Whether you'll try for the goal that's afar.
Or just be contented to stay where you are.[43]

Maximize Your Disability

These 700 Benjamites transformed their disability into an incredible ability. The Bible says they could throw stones with a sling and hit a hair. Their proficiency was the result of a great deal of practice. In biblical times they would take a horse hair from the tail or mane, tie a rock to it and then hang it from a branch.

These guys could actually sling a stone and hit a hair at a distance of fifty yards, slinging it at seventy miles an hour! Remember that they were not naturally left-handed. They were born right-handed. Because of a wound in battle they became disabled, only able to use their left hand. Not wanting to give up their place in the battle, they practiced long and hard until they were skilled marksmen with the sling. They maximized their disability and made it work for them.

Do you have any idea what it would take for you to be able to convert from what you did all your life and switch to something else? They embraced the change that had been imposed upon them and enabled themselves to serve in a new capacity.

What do you do when your routine is interrupted? Everybody can serve God when life is a bed of roses. Your business is growing. You and your wife are on a honeymoon everyday. The kids are behaving and doing well in school. You have money. You go on vacations. You have a wonderful home. Everything is so perfect. You are happy and enjoying your idyllic life.

Now, let's reverse this. What happens with your PG life when it becomes R-rated? How do you respond when the waves rock your yacht and trouble knocks on the door of your mansion?

Your business is facing bankruptcy. There is no more money for vacations and the luxuries that you have grown accustomed to are disappearing. Your marriage is in trouble. Your props have been knocked away and you are left hanging over a cliff.

Will you let your trouble *crush* you or *complete* you? Will you whine and complain and say that life is not fair? Or will you lift up your head and choose to make your troubles serve you in order to make you better?

When the going gets tough, the tough get going! Tough times are not for the weak at heart. I have discovered that my weaknesses are transformed into strength through the tough times. Leaders are born for adversity. The late Ronald Reagan (1911-2004), 40th President of the United States, described the actions of true leadership in this insightful way, "A leader, once convinced a particular course of action is the right one, must have the determination to stick with it and be undaunted when the going gets tough." [44]

Our wounds do not define us. What we do with our wounds is what defines us. Determination in the face of adversity is a characteristic of every great leader. They do not allow failure, opposition, handicaps or trials to deter them. They take all the struggles, all the disappointments, disillusionments, and depression and throw them in the face of the enemy.

They refuse to allow their disabilities to become excuses. Someone once said that excuses are the nails used to build a house of failure. The day that you stop making excuses is the day that the sun will begin to shine in your life. True leaders focus their attention on answers, not excuses.

These 700 wounded warriors from the tribe of Benjamin could have made excuses about their handicap. Instead they made a decision to convert their liability into ability. That conversion was not easy. It took long hours of practice and commitment to the goal. They refused to grow weary in the process.

> Your scars can become stars that will guide others through their own storms in life.

That is one of the things that I love about my work. Over the years I have watched hundreds of young people transform their weaknesses into strengths. I have been amazed at the strength it takes for a drug addict to turn his back on a life of drugs. They have become a sign to others that life without drugs is possible. I have watched as girls who have been victims of abuse rise out of the sorrow of shame and become warrior women of God. I have watched these wounded ones become heroes of faith, all for the glory of God. They turned their sorrow into joy and their weaknesses into strength.

Once evening I was in Ohio signing books and just having fun talking to people in the line. An elderly lady approached me and I could tell that she wanted to say something. I told her that I would be with her in a second. When I finished I went over to her and listened to her story. She told me that when her husband was alive he used to watch me on television all the time. She explained that he wasn't a fan of television evangelists, but he sure liked me. She went on to say, "There was always something about how you talked about the kids in New York that just made sense to him. It wasn't like the other stuff that he saw."

She said he often told her that when he died, he did not want his war medals to go to their kids. "You can do whatever you want with the car, the house, the money. Split it up and give it to the kids when I am gone, but don't ever give my World War II medals to the kids." She always asked him why. He said, "Because they don't understand." And he continued, "Especially the Purple Heart. Young people today don't understand. They don't even know what it is, let alone what it takes to get one."

She continued, "Wanting to know what to do with those medals, I asked him what I should do with them. You know what he said?"

He said, "If you ever find somebody who knows about loyalty and cares more about somebody else than they do themselves, give it to them."

She explained that her husband had been shot twice pulling a couple of his guys out of a fire fight and did not want to dishonor their memory by frivolously giving the medals to someone who did not know the value of loyalty and sacrifice. He wanted those medals to be reserved for someone who understood what it's like to be wounded in a battle and still keep going.

Looking up at me she said, "I drove here because I heard you were preaching this morning and I wanted to give you my husband's Purple Heart. I would like to give this to you, because I think you understand what it means to be wounded in a battle. I think you know what it means to not quit. I think you know what it means to care." She concluded by saying, "Just make him proud."

Needless to say, I received those medals as a great honor. I knew what they had meant to him and what they would mean to me— medals that represented a guy who did not give up in the middle of the battle, a guy who wore the scars of war on his body.

It is my prayer that as you are reading this book, you will be motivated to continue on the journey that you have started. Believe that you can make it in spite of the wounds that have been inflicted upon your life. Make the right decision. Do not quit! The day of victory is right before you. Do not allow your disability to be a liability.

God is looking for "left-handed people" who He can use in His army. Your scars can become stars that will guide others through their own storms of life. Now is not the time to give up. Now is the time to press through your pain to your ultimate destiny. You were born for this very moment. Do not give up when you are so close to life's final conclusion.

Chapter 11

DID ABNER DIE
AS A FOOL?

A fool sees not the same tree that a wise man sees.[45]

IT WAS NOT LONG ago that I had a tragic conversation with a man in Texas. He had been in ministry most of his life. His service for God was not debatable. Somewhere along the way things happened and he is no longer in the ministry. He is now a used car salesman. There is nothing wrong with being a used car salesman. The problem is how he got to that place in life. As we were talking, I finally found a place where I could ask him what happened.

I asked him, "Looking back on your life at this point in time, what were some of the decisions you made that took you out of the ministry?" He went into some detail as he tried to answer that question. I have no desire to expose him in this book, but he did say something that rang a bell for me and it made sense.

Opening the conversation he said, "I made some very foolish decisions. There was a time in my life when I made bad choices." He continued by saying, "I acted like a fool. I lived like a fool. At that time of my life, I was a fool."

I was a fool. Those are very tough words to admit. Most people would not be willing to acknowledge that they were a fool. Most of us would shift the blame to other people or to our circumstances. Few are willing to place the blame squarely on their own shoulders.

> The great goal in life for all of us should be to grow out of our foolishness and to become wise.

A fool is one that is lacking in discernment and wisdom. Their vision is clouded by their ignorance. They cannot see as others. They are unable to process information in a way that brings them to a reasonable conclusion. They get lost in the details and are easily deceived. A wise man simplifies the complex, while a fool complicates the simple. A fool is easily parted with his money because he is the object of every scam and the trickery of deceitful people.

Fools have no regard for the future and are driven by their emotions. Fools act without thinking and without regard for others. The great goal in life for all of us should be to grow out of our foolishness and to become wise. Some people never learn. Abner was one of the fools who never learned.

The Foolishness of Abner

Abner was a warrior, but he was a foolish warrior. As an uncle of King Saul, Abner was the commander in chief of the armies of the king. He was a man of great power and influence. We should never confuse power with wisdom.

It was Abner who first introduced David to King Saul. Abner remained loyal to Saul, and after Saul was killed in battle, he established Saul's only surviving son Ishbosheth as king. Eventually a crisis developed between Isbosheth and Abner with the result that Abner switched his allegiance to David, bringing all of Israel with him.

Joab, David's nephew and captain of his army, did not trust Abner. It was Abner who had killed his younger brother during the wars between and David and Ishbosheth. Abner was finally killed by Joab to avenge the death of his brother.

> *And David said to Joab, and to all the people that were with him, Rend your clothes, and gird you with sackcloth, and mourn before Abner. And king David himself followed the bier. And they buried Abner in Hebron: and the king lifted up his voice, and wept at the grave of Abner; and all the people wept. And the king lamented over Abner, and said, Died Abner as a fool dieth? Thy hands were not bound, nor thy feet put into fetters: as a man falleth before wicked men, so fellest thou. And all the people wept again over him.*
>
> —2 SAMUEL 3:31-34

At Abner's funeral, David asked this penetrating question, "Did Abner die as a fool?" In the context of the question we find our answer. Yes, Abner died as a fool. Abner was unable to see that the future belonged to David. He fought against God's plans for Israel. He had his own designs for power and continuously tried to position himself in a place where the power would be in his hands. His only concern was for himself. He acted selfishly, irrationally and foolishly.

The word "fool" is used seventy times in Proverbs alone.

> *Let a bear robbed of her whelps meet a man, rather than a fool in his folly.*
>
> —PROVERBS 17:12

> *A fool's mouth is his destruction, and his lips are the snare of his soul.*
>
> —PROVERBS 18:7

Answer not a fool according to his folly, lest thou also be like unto him.

He that sendeth a message by the hand of a fool cutteth off the feet, and drinketh damage.

—Proverbs 26:6

The Bible exposes the way of the fool, casting him in the light of his ignorance, ambition, folly and reckless living. Abner made certain choices in his life that rendered him on the wrong side. He should have realized that God was with David and cast his lot with the chosen one. Abner was foolish in his relationship with Joab. He should have submitted himself to Joab and made things right.

Finally, he should have understood the law regarding the cities of refuge, having been a civil leader for many years. Having killed Joab's brother, he could have fled to one of those cities and remained safe for the remainder of his life. Like too many he disregarded the words of God that are spoken for our safety and our security. Abner's foolishness and arrogance got him killed.

The Cities of Refuge

Under the Mosaic Code if a man accidentally killed someone then he could flee to the closest city of refuge. These cities were created under the Law as a place of asylum, protecting the offender from the blood-revenge. Blood-revenge was a very common practice in biblical times—an eye for an eye, a tooth for a tooth, and a life for a life. If a family member was killed by the hand of another, accidental or not, the kinsman considered it a duty to avenge him by killing the slayer.

Joab had the right to avenge his brother's death, even though it had taken place during battle. Those were the ancient ways. Abner was aware of this but in his foolishness, he did not flee to one of these cities.

In those days if you killed someone but you got to a city of refuge before their brother, cousin, or uncle could get to you, then you were safe. Just stepping inside the gate assured your safety. No one could kill you once you are inside the walls of the city of refuge (see Numbers 35).

Some say that it was generally maintained that originally every altar or sanctuary in the land could extend its protection to anyone who had unintentionally taken the life of another. But in order to more firmly secure this Law, six cities were established as cities of refuge (Numbers 35:6). They were located throughout the kingdom so that no matter where you lived in the land you were no more than one half day's journey from a city of refuge.

The Bible goes on to say that the Law provided safe refuge for that person for as long as the high priest lived in that city of refuge. As long as that high priest was alive, you could stay there and have refuge and be safe.

Three of the cities were located on one side of Jordan and three on the other. No river rolled between him and his place of safety. All of them stood in plains so that the person seeking refuge had no hill to climb. Near each city (except Bezer, which required no further mark, being seen afar on the long, spacious heath) stood a hill that served the purpose of an ensign to guide the guilty man and to invite him to the refuge.

Christ is considered to be a type or representative of the ancient city of refuge. Those who have sinned may flee to Him and find safety from the avenger, Satan. Andrew Alexander Bonar (18810-1892), the famous Scottish preacher, wrote a sermon on the cities of refuge. He concluded this sermon with these dramatic words:

> But like the saved man-slayer who dared not be found beyond
> the gate of the city until the High Priest had gone to glory
> (Num. 35:25), they dare not for an hour go out of their place

of safety. They abide in Christ. However holy they become, whatever reputation they have gained, however honoured and distinguished for spiritual attainments, they abide in Christ alone. Their first security was found in Him, and it is their security to the last. Though laden with the fruits of righteousness, and filled with all the graces of the Spirit, they depend for safety on the enclosing wall of their city of refuge, as much as does the sinner that only yesterday came in. And so they will remain till their High Priest enter upon 'his glorious rest' (Isa. 11:10); and then they shall share with Him in that joy, each one receiving his inheritance and possessing an unchanging love.[46]

There are further applications of the spiritual truth to the cities of refuge as you look deeper at each city. The names of the cities have tremendous theological and practical implications to us today. As I started researching these cities, I uncovered truths that will have critical importance to today's leaders. These buried truths are found in the Hebrew translation for each city.

Bezer—The Place of Strength

Bezer was set apart by Moses for the Reubenites and located in the "plain country" (or table-land, Mishor) East of the Jordan, and later assigned to this tribe by Joshua (Deut. 4:43; Josh 20:8). The same city was assigned by lot as a place of residence to the children of Merari of the Levite tribe (Joshua 21:36; 1 Chronicles 6:63, 78).

The word *Bezer* means "stronghold." A stronghold in biblical times was a fortified city built to withstand the attacks of the enemy. The city was usually surrounded by high walls and often built on a steep hill or in the cleft of a mountain. Solomon said that "the name of the LORD is a strong tower: the righteous runneth into it, and is safe" (Proverbs 18:10).

The wise man knows there is no
security in himself.

The spiritual implications of this truth are enormous. If you can come into that city, and if you can get to that place in Christ you will be safe. The fool believes in his own ability to save himself, but the wise person knows there is no security in himself. He seeks the security that is found in Christ. He alone is the only safe zone that is truly secure from the avenger.

The choice is yours to make. Will you seek the place of security provided by the work of Christ, or will you seek your own way? The ground you are standing on determines the security you seek in life. The issue is not what you have done. The issue is who you will trust.

Americans always want to know where you are from. People in the South think and talk differently than people in the Northeast. West Coast people are a different breed than those from the Midwest. Your culture, language and mindset are developed and impacted by where you were raised as a child.

Here is an important truth. I am not so much interested in where you are from as I am interested in where you are now. You may have had a horrible past. You were in places of darkness and despair. You hid in alleyways and crack houses. Some of those who read this book are from religious backgrounds, while others came from heathen backgrounds. Some were raised in great wealth while others were raised in poverty. Here is my point. It does not matter to me what your background is. I want to know where you are right now.

Are you still stuck in the past of religiosity, addiction abuse, and struggling with your shame and guilt? Or, have you fled to the city of refuge, the city that is a stronghold. Are you on the lam, or are you in the Lamb?

Golan—The Place of Separation

Golan was a city in the territory allotted to Manasseh in Bashan, the most northerly of the three cities of refuge east of the Jordan (see Deuteronomy 4:43). It was assigned to the Gershonite Levites (Joshua 21:27). It was a great and important city in its day and a place of rescue from the blood avengers. In his book, The *Antiquities of the Jews,* the important apologist of the Roman world for the Jewish people and culture, Josephus (AD 37-c. 100) speaks of Golan as the city destroyed by Alexander the Great.

That word *Golan* means "separated." As Christians we are called to come out from the filth of this world. We are called to live a separated life.

> *Wherefore come out from among them, and be ye separate, saith the Lord, and touch not the unclean thing; and I will receive you.*
>
> —2 Corinthians 6:17

We talk about living the separated life as Christians, but do we really understand what that means?

I don't think it means living in cloistered communities where we all do our religious thing. How can we *reach* the world if we do not *reach out* to the world? Being separate means that we separate ourselves from the *psyche* and the *pleasures* of the world.

We have all read of the surgeries that have taken place on Siamese twins conjoined at the head. Why is it worth the risk of going through this delicate surgery? The reason is simple—to offer them a better life. Being conjoined at the head limits the life that the two can live. It offers the possibility of living a separate life.

If you are conjoined to the world at the head, you have taken on the mindset of the world. You are under the influence of humanistic thinking that is in opposition to the mind of Christ. That is why Paul reinforces the need to have the mind of Christ.

> The natural man receiveth not the things of the Spirit of God: for they are foolishness unto him: neither can he know them, because they are spiritually discerned. But he that is spiritual judgeth all things, yet he himself is judged of no man. For who hath known the mind of the Lord, that he may instruct him? but we have the mind of Christ.
> —1 Corinthians 2:14-16

Paul makes a huge distinction between the wisdom of this world and the wisdom of God. There cannot be any peaceful coexistence. The wisdom of this world must be rejected and the wisdom of God must be embraced. We must be willing to separate ourselves from the wisdom of this world, no matter what kind of package it comes in. Spiritual judgment and discernment is not possible to those who will not reject the world's mindset and philosophy.

> The pleasures of this world are a daily attraction and once you are in the vice grip of their tentacles, you are trapped.

Also, we must separate ourselves from the pleasures of this world. Some people get this; some never will. There is a time when you have to put away childish things. The party life must be abandoned. The pleasures of this world are a deadly attraction and once you are in the vice grip of their tentacles, you are trapped.

Golan means separation—separation from the world and all that it has to offer. The only safe place is "in Christ." He is your place of security, where you are protected from the trickery of men with all their worldly philosophies, riotous acts and moral corruption.

Hebron—The Place of Fellowship

Hebron was originally a Canaanite royal city before it became one of the principle centers of the Tribe of Judah and one of the six traditional cities of refuge. The Bible account gives various conflicting identities to the owners of the city before Israelite settlement. At times Hebron is Amorite (Genesis 13:18), or Hittite (Genesis 23) and elsewhere Canaanite (Joshua 10:5-6).

Like Jerusalem, 23 miles to the north, the ancient city of Hebron stirs deep religious and political passions, and has been the scene of conflict between Jews and Arabs for much of the last century. It is mentioned in the Bible as being the site of Abraham's purchase of the Cave of the Patriarchs from the Hittites, in a narrative that some recent historians regard as constituting a late "pious prehistory" of Israel's settlement. In settling here, Abraham made his first covenant. Hebron, which rises 3,050 feet (926 meters) above sea level, has a long and rich Jewish history.

It was one of the first places where the Patriarch Abraham resided after his arrival in Canaan. King David was anointed in Hebron, where he reigned for seven years. Initially as a vassal of the Philistines and anointed by the men of Judah, David gradually extended his authority over a wider area, until he was able to incorporate the remnants of Saul's kingdom with the capture of Jerusalem, where he was subsequently anointed king of the Kingdom of Israel.[47]

The Hebrew word *Hebron* is derived from the Hebrew word for "friend" (*haver*), a description for the Patriarch Abraham, who was considered to be the friend of God. It signifies fellowship and friendship.

The key to all spirituality is friendship and fellowship. Abraham became a great man and his greatness was in the fact that he was a friend of God. You will not make it in this life unless you have fled to the city that is called fellowship. In that city, *experiences with*

God trump *knowledge of* God. It is not enough to know Him. You must experience life with Him.

It is not enough to have friends who are Christians. It is not enough to come from a Christian home. It is not enough to graduate from Bible college. You have to have your own relationship with God. You have to have fellowship with Him yourself. You cannot live the Christian life vicariously through others. It will never work.

That's why Elijah never did get it. People think Elijah was the greatest thing since sliced bread. I get into these big theological debates, because I don't believe Elijah was the hotshot prophet/man of God that many others seem to think he was. I think he blew it. First Kings 19 tells the story. God spoke to me in a what? In a silent voice, a silent voice, not the still small voice. The better rendition of that text is, "A silent voice." See, when you really know God, He doesn't have to speak to you in an audible voice.

Technically if you know me I shouldn't even have to talk to you in an audible voice. But most people don't know me, so I have to talk in an audible voice. If you knew me, all you would have to do is look at me and you would know my nature. You would know where I'm going. You would know what I like and dislike. You would know what I expect.

You learn these things when you know someone. But if you don't know somebody, then they are constantly forced to have to speak to you, to have to exhort you. Sometimes chastise you. Sometimes rebuke you. Why? Because you don't know them. You really don't know them. See, and that's why we still struggle in our relationships with God, because we don't know Him.

And any man reading this who is married knows there's a huge difference between the audible voice of the wife and the inaudible voice of the wife. And it's a wise man who learns the technique of the inaudible, because if it has to go to audible, it ain't pretty. I'm pretty sure you understand exactly what I'm saying.

God tried to speak to him in the silent voice, but Elijah never got it. Consequently, he had to be taken away, because he was no longer of any use. And it took four men to do the job that Elijah was supposed to do. But because Elijah didn't get it, others had to be picked.

Kedesh—The Place of Holiness

Kedesh was one of the southernmost cities of Judah close to the border of Edom in the South (Joshua 15:23). It might have been Kedesh-Barnea where Israel camped during their sojourn in the wilderness. It was once a fenced city of the tribe of Naphtali and one of the cities of refuge (see Joshua 19:37; Judges 4:6). It was originally a Canaanite royal city (Joshua 12:22) and was the residence of Barak, one of the judges of Israel (Judges 4:6).

From the meaning of its name we gather that it was a sanctuary from old times. It was therefore a place of asylum and only preserved its ancient character in this respect when chosen as one of the cities of refuge.[48]

> Confronted with the awesome holiness of God, there is no other appropriate human response than to fall down.

Kedesh means "holy" and therefore signifies that it is a holy place. It is made holy by the *Presence* of God in that place. It is not because there is something special about the ground that exists in that region. Whenever God's presence appears everything becomes sanctified. It was God's presence that made the ground holy. "Who is like unto thee, O LORD, among the gods? Who is like thee, glorious in holiness, fearful in praises, doing wonders?" (Exodus 15:11) The God of Israel was unique among all the other gods of Canaan. He was and is a holy God. There is no god like our God.

When King Uzziah died Isaiah was thrown into turmoil until he saw the Lord.

In the year that king Uzziah died I saw also the LORD sitting upon a throne, high and lifted up, and his train filled the temple.
—ISAIAH 6:1

While casting his eyes upon the Lord, he cried out, "Woe is me?" When we enter through the doors into the city of refuge that is called Kedesh, we are confronted with the awesome holiness of God. There is no other appropriate human response but to fall down. It took only one glimpse of the holiness of God, and Isaiah was reduced to his knees in utter awareness of his own unholiness.

Isaiah was a great prophet of God, but he shrunk into humility and recognition of who he was in the presence of this great God whom he served. Before Isaiah could get ready for the ministry, his sin and guilt needed to be atoned.

You go to Kedesh. You go to the holy place. It is at Kedesh that we are cleansed in the presence of a holy God. Inside that city of refuge there is healing, forgiveness and cleansing. It is a place where the enemy of your soul cannot accuse you.

Preachers have told me that because of their failure, there is no longer any forgiveness for them. What a horrible place to be—outside the one gate that can give you the forgiveness you desperately require. Yes, it is a holy place but it is also an accepting place where God receives you in order that He might forgive and heal you. You will die if you don't get to that city. Kedesh is for you, but you have to make your way there. You have to turn your back on your pride and run to that city of holiness.

Kedesh is always there. It never leaves. There are those who leave its gates and wander away. They never get back because of their shame. It makes no sense. The place of healing is there and it awaits them. All they have to do is return to the city that was made for them.

Ramoth—The Place of Exaltation

Ramoth in Gilead (or Ramothgilead) was a town in Gilead that was included in the territory of the Israelite tribe of Gad and about 25 miles east of the Jordan River (Joshua 20:8). It was at Ramothgilead in the battle with Syria that Ahab was killed. Elijah sent one of the sons of the prophets to Ramothgilead to anoint Jehu as king of Israel (2 Kings 9:1).

Ramoth means "exalted." Ramoth is the place where God was exalted by the praises of His people as King David sang.

> *Let them praise the name of the LORD: for his name alone is excellent; his glory is above the earth and heaven.*
> —PSALM 148:13

God is elevated above all the earth. He is lifted up by His character, by His nobility, and by the worship of His people. All that He is lifts Him up above all that we are. His glory and His majesty set Him apart from all of His creation. However, He sent His Son to us in order that we might join Him in those heavenly places.

> *And I, if I be lifted up from the earth, will draw all men unto me.*
> —JOHN 12:32

In His resurrection, Christ has lifted us with Him. We are now in heavenly places exalted in His glory. In Ephesians chapters one and two, we are told that we have been raised up into heavenly places with Christ. We were raised by the magnetic and majestic power of Christ. We have been lifted up out of the natural realm and elevated into a spiritual realm of reality. How did it happen? It happened by a power greater than any known power in the history of the world. The whole power of His resurrection and ascent to glory has lifted up all those who believe into that realm with Him.

When He got exalted, we got exalted. In that heavenly realm everything looks different. Our theology is rearranged. Our philosophy is corrected. Our faith is strengthened. Our hope is renewed. Our life is changed.

That place exists for you. You can be brought into a place of spiritual intuitiveness. You can be brought into a place of fellowship. You can be brought into a place of spiritual understanding where you realize that the battle has already been won.

> When we are faced with an enemy that is greater than us, we should flee to that exalted place rather than trying to fight the enemy.

I have a sermon called, "A Cat Can't Fly." The whole premise of the message was simply this, a bird is not going to go up to a cat and smack him in the mouth. A bird is smart enough to know that doesn't work. If the cat should see the bird hopping around on the ground, it will chase after it.

What does the bird do? It certainly does not turn around and fight the cat. The bird flies somewhere the cat cannot go. He goes to a higher place. Sometimes the bird is smarter than humans. When we are faced with an enemy that is greater than us, we should flee to that exalted place rather than trying to fight the enemy. The battle has already been won, but we go to that place where the battle is secure.

When you choose to live in that exalted place, the heavenly place, you don't mess around fighting the old battles. Don't fight the battle by yourself. I have seen drug addicts healed in a moment of time.

I have seen alcoholics delivered immediately. How? They got into that high place, that secret place in the heavens.

They were lifted up into that rarified heavenly air and were healed by the power of the risen Christ. There is healing in the exalted place. There is deliverance in the exalted place. There is victory in the exalted place. Go to Ramothgilead. He is there for you.

Shechem—The Place of Safety

Shechem was located in the Hill Country of Ephraim (Joshua 20:7) at the base of Mount Gerizim on its northeastern side. This ancient city was situated at the northern terminus of what is now called "The Patriarch's Highway" that followed the watershed fifty miles south to Hebron. Shechem was about thirty miles north of Jerusalem and the city of Samaria was seven miles northwest. Shechem is strategically located at the most important crossroad in the central part of the country.[49]

Shechem was a place of altars and historical markers. It was at Shechem that Abram "built an altar to the Lord who had appeared to him...and had given that land to his descendants" (Genesis 12:6-7). The Bible states that on this occasion, God confirmed the covenant he had already made with Abram. Jacob's well was dug in the area of Shechem, and it was at Shechem that Israel buried the bones of Joseph (Joshua 24:32).

Shechem means "shoulder" and signifies a place of rest and security. Within the walls of Shechem is a place where you will find peace and protection. Everyone needs someone to lean on and that someone is the Lord. Leaning on His shoulder, we are at rest and we are secure. Other shoulders might betray us, but He will never leave us or betray us. When you feel like your burden is too heavy, there is One that you can lean on, so lean on Him.

The problem is that we are so used to carrying our own load that we never think to let Him carry it. It is like the woman on the subway. She'd been carrying a big ole bag, a heavy bag. She got on the train and yet she was still carrying her load. Somebody leaned over and said, "You can put it down now. Let the train carry it."

She was so used to carrying it even when she didn't have to. After a while you get so used to carrying the load—the burden—that you don't know how to live without a weight on your shoulder. You get so used to carrying the struggles in your life that you think that's the only way you can ever live. I'm here to tell you that it is not the way to live. There is a place of rest for you where you don't have to carry the weight—where shame is erased by God's grace and sin is eradicated by Jesus' blood.

I have noticed that there are two kinds of people—people with problems and problem people. There is a huge difference. I have no problem dealing with people's problems. I do have a struggle dealing with problem people.

I'll sit and talk with you all day about your problems, but if you're just a person who doesn't want to go to the city (of refuge) then no amount of talking will help you. All you want to do is talk about your problem. You don't want the solution. You want sympathy, not healing. Don't be addicted to your problems. Run to the city where you can be relieved of your heavy burdens.

The cities do not go to the people. The city of refuge awaits you but to get there you have to take the first step and start the journey. If you feel distant from God, guess who moved? He didn't move. He said I will never leave you. In order to get to the right place you have to move. You're over here carrying the burden by yourself. You're over here struggling. You're over here in this drama. You're over here still caught up in the same old habits and issues because you chose not to go to city of refuge. It's close enough so that you can get there. What are you doing here outside the city?

Did Abner Die as a Fool

And when Abner was returned to Hebron, Joab took him aside in the gate to speak with him quietly, and smote him there under the fifth rib, that he died, for the blood of Asahel his brother. So Joab, and Abishai his brother slew Abner, because he had slain their brother Asahel at Gibeon in the battle. And they buried Abner in Hebron: and the king lifted up his voice, and wept at the grave of Abner; and all the people wept. And the king lamented over Abner, and said, Died Abner as a fool dieth?
—2 Samuel 3:27, 30, 32-33

Abner had reached the city of Hebron. He was safe within the walls of that ancient city of refuge. Joab set a trap for him and enticed him to the gate. Joab understood that he could not kill Abner inside the gate. He had to get him to the gate. Once he got him to the gate, he and Abishai, his brother, slew Abner and avenged the blood of their family.

Did he die as a fool? Yes, he did. He allowed himself to be coaxed away from the place of safety and security. He didn't stay in the place where he knew there was safety. He didn't stay in the place that was provided for him. He had no regard for the structure that was set up for his protection. He got careless about his life.

The cities of refuge are there for us. Christ is our life. He is our strength. He is our holiness. He is our exaltation. He is our safety. If we do not separate ourselves from the world and live in fellowship with Him, then we position ourselves in a very dangerous place.

If you get taken out because you just allow yourself to get so tired that you don't think you can carry the load anymore that is a sad story. If you allow your shame and guilt to paralyze you so that you don't run to the city, then it becomes your fault. God has done all that He can do to protect and exalt you, but you have to come to Him.

Don't play the part of the fool like Abner! Allow yourself to be drawn to the safe place by the power of His resurrected life and glorious grace. Lay your burden down at the crossroads and make your way to the city prepared for you by the blood of the Lamb.

You must learn that there are consequences in life that are determined by your choices and decisions. You did not get to the place where you are by accident. Your decisions in life guided you to either the right city or the wrong city.

A place has been created for you, but you have to decide if that is what you want. If you are tired of the enemy's harassment, if you are sick of the burden you are carrying, and if you want to let go of your shame and guilt, then here is the answer. Flee to the city! In that city (of refuge) you will encounter the power of His resurrection where the curses on your life will be reversed and the weight on your shoulders will be eliminated and your enemies will be exterminated.

Chapter 12

STAY IN THE HOUSE

One of the annoying things about believing in free will and individual responsibility is the difficulty of finding somebody to blame your problems on. And when you do find somebody, it's remarkable how often his picture turns up on your driver's license.[50]

ONE OF THE MOST famous stories in the Bible is told by Jesus in Luke 15—the story of the Prodigal Son. The Prodigal Son account follows the parables of the Lost Sheep and the Lost Coin. The context of these three stories about the lost is Jesus' response to the Pharisees' complaint: "And the Pharisees and scribes murmured, saying, This man receiveth sinners, and eateth with them" (Luke 15:2). It is a story of tragedy turned into triumph, finalized by the love of an amazing father. It is the gospel within the Gospels.

B.B. Warfield (1851-1921), that great theologian of the early 20th century, described the artistic and spiritual beauty of this story with these articulate words: "It is the pearl and crown of all the parables of Scripture. Nothing could exceed the chaste perfection of the narrative, the picturesque truth of its portraiture, the psychological delicacy of its analysis. Here is a gem of story-telling, which must be pronounced nothing less than artistically perfect, whether viewed in its general impression, or in the elaboration of its details. We must add to its literary beauty, however, the preciousness of the lesson it conveys before we account for the place it has won for itself in the hearts of men. In this setting of fretted gold, a marvel of the artificer, there lies a priceless jewel; and this jewel is displayed to such advantage by its setting that men cannot choose but see and admire."[51]

Unfortunately we have come to associate this classic story as warning for the backslider. It is so much deeper in spiritual significance than a simple story of what happens when one goes astray. The whole story is packed with dynamic treasures detailing the distress of paradise lost and the delight of paradise regained. It is a story of lost and found, repentance and reception, a son's rebellion and a father's love.

> And he said, A certain man had two sons: And the younger of them said to his father, Father, give me the portion of goods that falleth to me. And he divided unto them his living. And not many days after the younger son gathered all together, and took his journey into a far country, and there wasted his substance with riotous living. And when he had spent all, there arose a mighty famine in that land; and he began to be in want. And he went and joined himself to a citizen of that country; and he sent him into his fields to feed swine. And he would fain have filled his belly with the husks that the swine did eat: and no man gave unto him.
>
> And when he came to himself, he said, How many hired servants of my father's have bread enough and to spare, and I perish with hunger! I will arise and go to my father, and will say unto him, Father, I have sinned against heaven, and before thee, and am no more worthy to be called thy son: make me as one of thy hired servants. And he arose, and came to his father. But when he was yet a great way off, his father saw him, and had compassion, and ran, and fell on his neck, and kissed him. And the son said unto him, Father, I have sinned against heaven,

*and in thy sight, and am no more worthy to be called thy son.
But the father said to his servants, Bring forth the best robe, and
put it on him; and put a ring on his hand, and shoes on his feet:
And bring hither the fatted calf, and kill it; and let us eat, and
be merry: For this my son was dead, and is alive again; he was
lost, and is found. And they began to be merry.*

—LUKE 15:11-24

Stay in the House

Father's house—the source of inspiration for all the biblical rights
and for men and women throughout the history of Christianity.
David often spoke of the love he had for the house of God.

> *LORD, I have loved the habitation of thy house, and the
> place where thine honour dwelleth.*

—PSALM 26:8

> *One thing have I desired of the LORD, that will I seek after;
> that I may dwell in the house of the LORD all the days of my life,
> to behold the beauty of the LORD, and to enquire in his temple.*

—PSALM 27:4

The house that David so passionately speaks of is not to be
confused with heaven or with church. It is not a place reserved for
those after they die and it is not a building that we go to on Sundays.
The depth of David's love was reserved for the house that represented the Father's *presence*. In other words when you are under
the umbrella of His house, you are under the protection of His *presence*. There is no greater place in the world. It is not a physical place
located on some holy ground. It is not a sacred place like Lourdes,
or Fatima or even Jerusalem. It is not a place that you go to visit.
The house that David spoke of was the house of His *presence*—the
presence sought by all of God's great leaders.

It is not a place that we visit. David talked about dwelling in the *presence*, taking up residence in the place where God's presence is manifest. It is not simply attending church on Sunday, enjoying worship and hearing a good sermon. That is **not** what David was talking about.

He was talking about staying in the house.

He was implying that there is a place where we were called to live. It is to be our place of residence, not our vacation home. It is our life, not our recreation. It is our pursuit, not our hobby. It is not a 9 to 5 job. It is the totality of our life.

As Brother Andrew (1928-), the famous Bible smuggler/ missionary taught us, it is a lifestyle. "There is not in the world a kind of life more sweet and delightful, than that of a continual conversation with God; those only can comprehend it who practice and experience it" said Brother Lawrence (1614-1691), French Carmelite monk, best known for his timeless Christian classic, *The Practice of the Presence of God.*[52]

It's a lifestyle, my friend. You dwell there. You live there. You desire nothing else, because you know that the *presence* changes you, motivates you, enlivens you, protects you, encourages and inspires you. My life is better when I'm in the house. I deal with things better when I'm in the house.

In His house He prepares a table for us in the presence of our enemies. He is the Master Chef, and His meals are like nothing you have ever had before—enchanting appetizers, delectable cuisine, and delightful desserts. While you are feasting at the table of the Lord, your enemies look on in disgust.

Give Me My Inheritance

The story does not tell us the reason why the younger son wanted to leave his father's house. It is clear that there was no reasonable reason for him to leave. There were a lot of reasons for him to *stay in the house.* There was no lack inside the house. In fact, there was great abundance in the house. There was security in the house. There was joy in the house. There were no problems in the house. Even the lowest slave was graciously cared for.

The young man says, "Give me my portion now." He wants to run his own life. He wants his independence. He wants control. He thinks he can handle it without Papa. "I can do this without listening to the old man. I've done this long enough."

Why leave? It is clear that he wanted to mark his own path in life, separate from his father. He believed he no longer needed his father's authority governing his life. He didn't need anyone looking over his shoulder. He wanted his freedom to exercise his independence. He wanted to take care of his own future, take control of his own destiny. He did not appreciate what he had in his father's house. His eyes were looking in the wrong direction—on the other side of the road. His imagination created a scenario where life would be better outside his father's house. Sadly, his imagination was a delusion.

> When you stand next those who are close to God, you will enjoy their blessing and favor.

He was blessed while he was in his father's house. He enjoyed wealth, respect and protection. I have often said that when you stand close to somebody who is close to God, you will enjoy their blessing and favor. There are young people who have come to this ministry in New York and have enjoyed the favor that comes from this place. They have received an opportunity to serve, to travel and to experience things that would be impossible in most places. The doors that open for me become open for them.

The younger son lost his perspective on this truth. No longer did he understand that being in his father's house gave him great favor and opportunities that others would never know. *He should have stayed in the house.*

Every now and then we look around, and we think we can do it. We can handle our life. We might not verbalize our thoughts, but they are there, present in our actions. We make our own decisions without consulting God. We choose to go places He never called us to. We begin to think that it is all about us. We become blinded by the spotlight and deceived by the accolades. The public place lures us away from the private place. I've watched multi-million dollar empires be destroyed in one week because somebody thought it was about them and their gifts and anointing.

The son fell into a subtle trap. He wanted the goods without the guidance. He thought that he could handle all that wealth without accountability. Here is one thing that I have learned in life: Goods without guidance leads to famine. There is nothing wrong with the goods, but when you choose to have the goods without guidance, you get into trouble.

Most people have fallen into trouble when they reject account-ability or surround themselves with "yes" people. All of us need accountability. We were never created to be the Lone Ranger. Even the Lone Ranger had Tonto.

Just look at the stories of people who suddenly come into wealth. The person who wins the lottery, the football star who lands his first huge contract—all that money without advice becomes corrupted by their inability to manage it. They reject the counsel of good advisers and before they know it, the money is all gone.

You need guidance. You need somebody with maturity who can guide you in the use of your inheritance. Only the fool rejects the counsel of the wise. The book of Proverbs is a book about the value of sound wisdom and counsel.

*Where no **COUNSEL** is, the people fall: but in the multitude of counsellors there is safety.*

—PROVERBS 11:14

*The way of a fool is right in his own eyes: but he that hearkeneth unto **COUNSEL** is wise.*

—PROVERBS 12:15

*Without **COUNSEL** purposes are disappointed: but in the multitude of counsellors they are established.*

—PROVERBS 15:22

*Hear **COUNSEL**, and receive instruction, that thou mayest be wise in thy latter end.*

—PROVERBS 19:20

When I was 26 years old, I made a wrong decision that I will pay for the rest of my life. I was told by three people, "Don't do this." But I was 26. I knew it all. I wasn't even smart enough to know I was stupid. I should have listened to that counsel. I should have stayed in the house.

The son would never have experienced famine in his father's house. But once he stepped outside the gate, he was confronted with things he had never expected—famine and poverty. When we find ourselves in a place of need, then we need to examine how we got there. God is not in trouble. You are, because you forsook proper counsel. You allowed your greed and visions of grandeur to lead you into places where God never called you. And then you wonder where God is.

The Prodigal spent his entire inheritance, and there came famine. Famine led to want. The word *want* literally means "lasciviousness." *Lasciviousness* means "unrestrained action." Credit cards produce unrestrained action. And we wonder why this country is in such financial trouble. The amount of debt accumulated by the government and by individuals has reached astronomical proportions and we can no longer bear the weight of that debt.

What is he to do? He has no money. Famine has hit. He has no experience in these matters. Jesus says that he joined himself to a citizen of that country. He became a slave of a heathen. His desire for wealth and independence led him far away from Father's house. It left him debt ridden. The ecstasy of independent living and acquiring new things eventually fashioned a noose around his neck. Enough is never enough.

King Solomon observed this phenomenon three thousand years ago when he wrote these words now found in the Bible: "The eye is not satisfied with seeing, nor the ear filled with hearing" (Ecclesiastes 1:8). Experiencing more and more pleasure will ultimately not give anybody the true success that brings happiness. Eventually you will become a slave of others—a slave of the heathen. The Prodigal's life has become a disaster. His fantasies have been transformed into nightmares.

His desire to find approval took him away from the *one* place where it could be found. His father's love allowed the son the freedom to pursue a search to far away places. Leaving home, the son found that the further he got away from the voice of Father's unconditional love, the stronger was the pull to a "distant country." His journey, as the story goes, eventually left him lost, lonely, loveless and digging for food in a pig pen.

Make Me Your Servant

In the midst of his despair and loneliness, the Prodigal remembers. There is nothing like the marvelous power of a loving memory! Remembering Father and home decided it for him. He was going back. It may never be the same, but at least he would be home.

> Our true home is the Presence of the Father, and He has left the light on while He waits for our return.

In his efforts to prove himself he had destroyed his life and brought much shame to the family name. Fortunately, his passion to return was more powerful than the shame that covered him. The memory of Father's house was strong, and its magnetic pull was working on the young man's heart.

Father has placed within each one of us an internal *photo album* that serves as a faithful reminder of a better place. This is the *original* case of homesickness and is a fundamental part of the human nature. Our collective memory tells us that our true home is the Presence of Father, and He has left the Light on while He waits for our return. Dutch-born Catholic priest and writer Henri Nouwen (1932-1996) described that longing in this way.

> The ongoing yearning of the human spirit, the yearning for a final return, an unambiguous sense of safety, a lasting home.... But beneath or beyond all that, 'coming home' meant, for me, walking step by step toward the One who awaits me with open arms and wants to hold me in an eternal embrace.[53]

He started thinking. We must get to the place where we turn off the radio and the television, the iPod and the laptop and shut down all those noises seeking to assuage our shame and guilt. This self-induced white noise simply drowns out the answers we are seeking. If you can get yourself into the Presence, you will hear His voice— the voice reminding you that you have a home waiting for you.

Our boy finally comes to his senses. A light is turned on, a light of enlightenment and revelation no man gave to him. Not welfare. No handouts. You know what I've learned? It took me awhile to learn this. Sometimes helping people isn't really helping them. I'm going to say that again. Sometimes helping people doesn't really help them. There are times that the only way people can learn is the hard way.

You see, eagles build their nests on high cliffs and in tall trees. The great heights at which the eagles build their nests represents the highest level of achievement that one can achieve in a life which focuses on good eating, exercise, discipline, respect, and self-control.

The story of the eagle is one of my favorites and fits so well in illustrating my point. Eagles build their nests high in crevices of the great mountains. These nests can sometimes reach ten feet in width. The nests are built of thorns on the outside and soft grasses and feathers on the inside. At the appropriate time the mother eagle hovers above the eaglets' nest and begins to flap those huge wings. The little eaglets are troubled by their mother's actions. As the flapping continues the soft feathers and grasses are blown away leaving only a bed of thorns. Now is the time for one of the most amazing events in nature to begin.

The mother eagle is not done yet. She actually begins kicking the baby eagle out of the nest of thorns. It has not yet learned to use its wings and scared and frightened, the baby falls toward the ground. Right before it looks like it is going to hit the ground, the father eagle flies under and catches the baby on his back. He soars back to the nest and starts the process all over again. At the last moment the father eagle flies under the falling baby and catches him on his back. Then the father eagle soars back up to the nest to deliver the baby eagle back to the nest.

For weeks the mother and father keep doing the same thing until the baby eagle finally flaps its wings enough to fly on its own.[54]

There is a time when we must leave the comfort of our nests and open our hearts to be and do greater and more wonderful things for ourselves and others.

Like eagles, we too have to learn many things to reach our full potential and live as we ought to live. There is a time when we must be challenged to leave the comfort of our nests and open our hearts (like the wings of an eagle) to be and to do greater and more wonderful things for ourselves and for others.

There comes a time when you have to grow up and sometimes the only way you can mature is through the struggles of life. If we are always being bailed out, we will never learn. Sometimes the spigot of assistance has to be turned off so we can learn that God is our only Source.

The Prodigal finally sees the light—life would be much better in his father's house. He realizes that daddy's servants are better off than he is right now. His downward spirals began with these words—*give me!* His journey home begins with these words—*make me!* He is being adjusted and changed from a selfish brat to a serving son. He knows he messed up. He knows he wasted his life and his inheritance. He does not deserve his father's mercy and he is willing to just be his dad's servant.

A Father's Love

Finally the light comes on. His mind and heart connects with reality. The love of his father is drawing him back home. He has fine-tuned his repentance speech. He knows what to do. He will tell father that he does not deserve his love and that he messed up his life. He will ask to simply be a servant in his father's house. That is all he will ask for.

The closer the son got to home, the clearer his memories became. He could seem to see father's face more clearly with each step he took and anticipation was growing. As he crested the hill upon which his home sat, he saw a figure get up from a rocking chair. He seemed to be peering intently in his direction. Suddenly, the person took off running toward him.

Father!

What he didn't know was that Father had been waiting every day since he had gone. Sitting on the front porch day after day, gazing longingly into the distance for his lost boy to return. As his father reached him and pulled him into a bear hug, the son started to give the speech he had so carefully prepared. "I'm not worthy! Make me as one of your servants." But his body was drawn into the arms of his father as he was lavished with hugs and kisses from his dad.

As both cried with sobs of thanksgiving and relief, the young man heard his father's tender words. "My son, my son, you've come home. You've come home!" No apologies necessary. No recriminations given. Just, "Let's have a party!"

Before he knew it, the father had put a ring on his finger, shoes on his feet, a robe around his shoulders, and was preparing a fatted calf. Was he dreaming? Was this really happening? Never in his wildest imaginations could he have dreamed such a scene.

Ring, Sandals, Robe and the Fatted Calf

Why did he give him a ring? Did he need jewelry? No. This was no ordinary ring. It was the family ring, a signet ring. The ring was a symbol of the rights that went along with the ring. With the ring you are more than a servant; you are a son. With that ring come privileges. The wayward son said, "I'll come back as a servant," but because he had learned from his mistakes and returned to his father, he got the ring. He was willing to give up his rights.

172

It would have been natural for the father to say, "Yeah, you better believe you'll give it up. You're an idiot! You're a knucklehead! You don't deserve to be my son." Not this father. This father is a father who loves his son in spite of his failures. The servant has had the benefit of living in the house, but the Prodigal had the privileges of a son. He finally learned the power of humility and was restored to his place as a son.

Because I travel so much, I qualify for a lot of privileges. Recently I stayed at a Hilton Hotel. I have a double-diamond VIP card. It is the result of all the times I have stayed in a Hilton. Not everyone gets that card. When I check into a Hilton, they roll out the red carpet. My double-diamond VIP card gets me into a private room, an executive lounge on the top floor. My swipe card opens the snack room. My swipe card opens the workout room. My swipe card opens the Jacuzzi room. That card brings special advantages.

With the ring the son got power and authority and you have the ring of Christ. It is not the Pope's ring. It is a real ring of authority given to you by the Father. You have power and authority as a son (daughter) of God.

The son was also given sandals. The sandals picture freedom. Slaves at that time were barefoot. And although the Prodigal wanted to be a servant, the father saw him as much more. He was a son, and his father cherished him greatly. In order to understand the importance of this gift you have to understand the ancient custom.

Now this was the manner in former time in Israel concerning redeeming and concerning changing, for to confirm all things; a man plucked off his shoe, and gave it to his neighbor: and this was a testimony in Israel.

—RUTH 4:7

In giving the son the shoes, he was declaring that things have changed. *You are no longer a stranger in my house. You have been redeemed and the sign that confirms our relationship is the shoes. Every time you look at your shoes, you will remember my love and the mercy I show to you this day.*

Ephesians 6 says that we are to have our feet shod with the gospel of peace. We are given the shoes of peace. The shoes represent reconciliation and the establishment of peace. The battle is over. My son is home, and the shoes represent the end of his rebellion and independence. He is now home.

Next the father put a robe on his son. The robe represents distinction, honor and nobility. Genesis 37:3 describes the coat of many colors that Jacob gave his favorite son, Joseph. Jacob was distinguishing his son Joseph from the other brothers. That's why there was such anger toward Joseph among his siblings. It separated him from his other brothers. God designed a priestly robe for Aaron. It was the robe of the High Priest—a robe of tribute and privilege. The robe gave him access into the *presence* of God.

The robe represents intimacy (Joseph's coat) and honor (Aaron's robe). In Christ we have been robed in intimacy and honor. A great sacrifice was paid for that robe—the blood of the Son. The robe is given with love and a desire to share with us the glories that he has with his Father. We have been invited into the house of the Lord where we are treated as royalty because of Christ.

Finally, there was a party. The fatted calf was killed and the celebration began. There will always be joy in the house of the Lord when a delinquent son comes home. The only thing the father wanted was his son. His place was at his side, not in the pig pen. No one knows the joy of the father when he is reunited with his son.

Everything's all right in my Father's house. The son is *home*. The celebration has begun. God does know how to throw a great party.

The son has learned his lesson. *Stay in the house.* Stay in His *presence.* Don't leave the place of His protection, His provision and His passion.

Chapter 13

SAME HUNGER, DIFFERENT HOUSE

Passion, it lies in all of us, sleeping... waiting... and though unwanted... unbidden... it will stir... open its jaws and howl. It speaks to us... guides us... passion rules us all, and we obey. What other choice do we have? Passion is the source of our finest moments. The joy of love... the clarity of hatred... and the ecstasy of grief. It hurts sometimes more than we can bear. If we could live without passion maybe we'd know some kind of peace... but we would be hollow... Empty rooms shuttered and dank. Without passion we'd be truly dead.[55]

I T WAS MAY 1954, at the Iffley Road Track in Oxford, England, when medical student Roger Bannister (1929-) became the first person in recorded history to run the mile in under four minutes. The historic event was watched by about three thousand spectators. It almost never happened because of winds up to twenty-five miles per hour prior to the event. But the winds died down and Bannister decided to run. Two other runners, Brasher and Chataway provided pacing while Bannister completed the race. Both went on to establish their own track careers. To the cheers of the crowd it was announced that Bannister had broken the barrier.

Until that moment in time everyone considered this feat impossible. Doctors said it could never be done. People who were in charge of athletic programs in those days said it would never happen. They all said that is was physically and humanly impossible to break the four-minute mile. The body could not take the strain imposed upon it to run a mile in less than four minutes.

In an interview Bannister made these comments, "I wanted this more than anything else in the world. He said, 'I was so hungry, I could taste it.'" The passion to break this record drove him to success. You can hear the passion reverberating in these quoted words by Bannister.

> The man who can drive himself further once the effort gets painful is the man who will win. I leapt at the tape like a man taking his last spring to save himself from the chasm that threatens to engulf him. We run, not because we think it is doing us good, but because we enjoy it and cannot help ourselves.[56]

All accomplishments in life require the assistance of others. No man is an island. One's life's work necessitates the efforts of others. Those two runners acting as pace setters helped Bannister reach his goal. Anyone who knows anything about long distance running knows that if you run behind someone, they create a pace and draft that assist the runners behind them.

Geese in their long distance flights use the same phenomenon. The lead geese break the power of the wind for those behind in the formation and those lead geese must be alternated in order to preserve stamina. Their "wind breaking" creates an aerodynamic that makes the flight much easier for those behind them.

In auto racing we see a similar drafting effect. Those who have watched racing will notice how closely the other racecars snuggle up to the one in front of them. The advantage of this approach is that the cars share the same "pocket of air," allowing them to travel a few miles an hour faster than they would be able to if they were driving separately. The concept is also called *slipstreaming* because the front car opens up a "passageway" through the air that trailing cars can then travel through at higher speed.

Encouragement is like a slipstream created by another that supports others in the race of life. When we applaud the efforts of others, acknowledge their successes, and encourage them in their pursuits, we will help them to succeed. When we all help one another, everybody wins.

Since Bannister broke the record, 167 others have broken that barrier. He made a way for others and so will you with every success you have in your life.

In 1980 inner-city urban works were almost non-existent in this country. And that's why everybody thought I would never succeed. Not only have we succeeded, we have duplicated our work all over the world. As with Bannister, I had the hunger and desire to do what others had never been able to do.

How hungry are you? Your hunger is in direct proportion to your accomplishments in life. There is no goal in life that is achievable without the burning fire of desire. Hunger is the key to motivation because motivation finds its strength in the passion of hunger. We create our own worlds through the passionate desire that drives our lives. Without that hunger we will remain in the cycle of conformity, letting others choose our lives for us.

Same Hunger, Different House

There was a certain man in Caesarea called Cornelius, a centurion of the band called the Italian band, a devout man, and one that feared God with all his house, which gave much alms to the people, and prayed to God alway. He saw in a vision evidently about the ninth hour of the day an angel of God coming in to him, and saying unto him, Cornelius. And when he looked on him, he was afraid, and said, What is it, Lord? And he said unto him, Thy prayers and thine alms are come up for a memorial before God. And now send men to Joppa, and call for one Simon, whose surname is Peter: He lodgeth with one Simon a tanner, whose house is by the sea side: he shall tell thee what thou oughtest to do.

—ACTS 10:1-6

The story of Cornelius offers us insight into God's purposes among the Gentiles. The salvation that Jesus brought to men would not be exclusively offered to the Jews but was meant to be for all men.

Cornelius was a Roman centurion stationed in the city of Caesarea. He was an unusual Gentile in that he embraced monotheism, the belief in one God, as opposed to the Greeks and Romans that served a whole pantheon of gods.

His belief in the one true God impacted his life. He was a moral man who did many good deeds for those around him, especially the poor. His entire household shared his faith in this one God.

Being a religious man it was his habit to engage himself in regular prayer to his God. Cornelius was hungry for God. He has been prepared for the coming events by his passion and purpose. He disciplined himself to focus on that passion for God. He knew there was something else that he had to have. There was something he wanted and didn't know how to get, but knew it was something he needed. He knew there was more. And he wanted everything that God had for him.

On one occasion while he was praying, an angel appeared to him. The appearances of angels will always signal something significant in the history of men. The angel told him that God had recognized his spiritual hunger and wanted him to send for a man named Peter who lived in the city of Joppa in the house of a man called Simon the tanner. It is possible that Cornelius was seeking God in the manner of the Old Covenant and most assuredly had not heard of the death or resurrection of Jesus. The angel's words would open a doorway for Cornelius to hear the message of Jesus.

A Roman Soldier and the Jewish Preacher

The other key figure in this story is Peter. Peter would be the key to Cornelius' hungry prayer. God knew exactly where the answer was for Cornelius. The answer was in Simon's home, south of present day Tel Aviv on the Mediterranean.

God knows where you are, as well. Physically, emotionally and spiritually, God knows where you are. Your friends may not know where you are. Your wife may not know where you are. Your husband may not know where you are. Your family may not know where you are. Your pastor may not know where you are. But God does know. This truth should bring you encouragement. Continue to pray. Continue to allow the hunger in your heart to be expressed in your words directed toward heaven. He will hear. He will answer.

These two guys lived in totally different worlds—a Jew and a Roman soldier. The Jews hated the Romans because of the occupation of their land. The Romans despised the Jews for their monotheistic beliefs and the resistance to their rule.

The Law created a wall between the Jew and the Gentile. Jews and Gentiles would never eat together, nor associate with each other. In fact, it was a rule that if a Gentile came to your house and did eat, you were required to break the plate. There was a prejudicial barrier that existed between these two groups of people.

Religious tradition is a hindrance to the purposes of God. Once it is embedded into the soul of our being it is hard to eradicate. I know a little bit about religious tradition. I was raised at a time when religious tradition was the practice of the day. The Pentecostals that I grew up among thought we were the only ones going to heaven. We had the Holy Ghost and the rest were doomed to Hell.

I have been around religious tradition so much that I can easily sniff out its putrid odor. I think there are certain biblical truths that you adhere to because they are absolutes. But I also believe that there are certain religious beliefs and practices that are simply traditional and not absolute. You aren't saved because of how you cut your hair, what kind of clothes you wear, or any other preference you cling to.

Throughout history, Jesus confronted religious tradition.

The great challenge of our day is to know the difference between a biblical absolute and a personal preference. Biblical absolutes are untouchable. Personal preferences can change. You get into problems when you make a biblical absolute into a preference or you establish a personal preference as an absolute.

Throughout his ministry on the earth Jesus confronted religious tradition. It seems that He purposely violated the laws of men in order to show them the higher law of love. The story of Jesus and the woman at the well is a relevant one.

There cometh a woman of Samaria to draw water: Jesus saith unto her, Give me to drink. (For his disciples were gone away unto the city to buy meat.) Then saith the woman of Samaria unto him, How is it that thou, being a Jew, askest drink of me, which am a woman of Samaria? for the Jews have no dealings with the Samaritans.

—JOHN 4:7-9

There were three issues with this woman. She was a Samaritan—a racial issue. The Samaritans were despised by the Jews and their religion was considered to be a counterfeit religion. Samaria was part of the northern kingdom that chose Baal over Jehovah. They were finally judged as the prophets declared by the Assyrian army. The Assyrians promoted the coming together of the heathen with the remaining Jews in the land. Israel viewed the Samaritans as half-breeds and rejected them.

Secondly, she was a woman—a gender issue. There were strict laws on the interactions between men and women in those days. Down through the ages women have too often been considered second-class citizens and their rights have often been abused.

Finally, she was an adulteress—a moral issue. She was guilty of sexual promiscuity and therefore to be avoided at all cost. No Jew would ever be in the presence of such a woman.

Jesus broke all the laws when he asked her for a drink of water. The woman was perplexed by His request. That simple request exposed all religious tradition and made it clear that the Gospel of Jesus was and is for all people.

We have our own issues in these days. I grew up on Central Avenue in Saint Petersburg, Florida. Central Avenue was the dividing line in town. All the black folks lived on the south side. All the white folks lived on the north side. Now there were no signs there, but everybody knew the rules didn't they? They were unspoken rules, yes, but they were there. Prejudice has created great walls that separate God's people.

There is a town in Western Orange County, Texas called Vidor. I was in Vidor one time. Until just recently there was a sign as you entered the city that said: "Welcome to Vidor, an All-White Community."

I was a guest in the home of a member of the Assembly of God Church in Vidor and of course, there was a picture hanging on the living room wall. If I hadn't seen it myself, I wouldn't have believed it!

It was an old black and white picture of the Ku Klux Klan hanging a black man. It was a beautifully framed photograph that they had decided to hang in their living room. I could hardly believe what I saw!

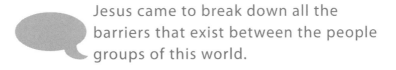

Jesus came to break down all the barriers that exist between the people groups of this world.

On another occasion I was in Texas signing books. Let me make it clear that I don't use this language, but this is what this guy said. This Texan came up to me and said, "I don't really care for those old niggers, but if you want to work with them, I'll pay you." A lot has been done to erase racial prejudice in this country, but, unfortunately, it still exists.

It is very difficult for me to deal with this kind of stupidity. I cannot tolerate racism, no matter what form it comes in. It is an abomination and an insult to the God we serve. Jesus came to break down all barriers that exist between the people groups of this world.

Now God had been preparing Cornelius for his divine appointment and at the same time, he was preparing Peter for this same divine appointment. You see Peter had his own issues. Peter was ensnared in his own religious trap. Cornelius did not have racial or religious issues. He had embraced the God of the Jews. Peter was the one who had the issue with the unclean Gentiles. He could not quite imagine a Church that could include Gentiles.

Hungry People Have Dreams

On the morrow, as they went on their journey, and drew nigh unto the city, Peter went up upon the housetop to pray about the sixth hour: And he became very hungry, and would have eaten: but while they made ready, he fell into a trance, and saw heaven opened, and a certain vessel descending unto him, as it had been a great sheet knit at the four corners, and let down to the earth: wherein were all manner of fourfooted beasts of the earth, and wild beasts, and creeping things, and fowls of the air. And there came a voice to him, Rise, Peter; kill, and eat. But Peter said, Not so, Lord; for I have never eaten any thing that is common or unclean.

—ACTS 10:9-14

Notice the difference between Cornelius's response and Peter's. At the moment that Cornelius received the angelic message, he sent a messenger to Peter. There was no hesitation. But Peter could not respond until he had confronted his traditions.

The narration says that when Peter was very hungry he fell into a trance. Just like the marathon runner Bannister, he was very hungry. Hungry people are the ones who have dreams.

> When things are looking their worst, hungry people will be driven toward the goal that is before them.

The question I leave for you is: How hungry are you? If you don't have a dream, maybe you aren't hungry enough. People who are not driven will not dream. If you have lost your passion it will produce dreamless nights.

God comes to the hungry.

Hungry people have the "eye of the tiger." When things are looking their worst, hungry people will be driven toward the goal that is before them.

How bad do you want to make a difference? How much do you want to see something happen? Those who are satisfied will never be among the successful. Driven people are successful people.

Nobel Prizewinner (in physics) Albert Einstein (1879-1955), known the world over for his theories of special and general relativity, published more than 300 scientific and over 150 non-scientific works. He is often regarded as the father of modern physics. Yet he once said that he had no talents—only passionate curiosity. That passionate curiosity was the energy that propelled him into the most dramatic discoveries of his time. Hungry people are dreamers. Hungry people are visionaries. Hungry people are passionate people. Hungry people accomplish things!

Prejudice of the Preconditioned

Peter's hunger led him into a dream. He saw a sheet come down and all these animals, all the unclean things held by four corners of a sheet. Now I don't think that Peter was necessarily prejudiced, but I do believe he was preconditioned.

There's a difference between prejudice, pre-judging and preconditioning. It is possible that our environment will precondition us to think and act in a certain way. This preconditioning is not necessarily a prejudice.

When I first came to New York, I saw that a lot of people were preconditioned to hate white people. They had projected all of their previous abuse toward white people. I think there are a lot of black leaders who have done great harm to the movement started by Dr. Martin Luther King.

In his most famous speech, "I Have a Dream," King said: *I have a dream that my four little children will one day live in a nation where they will not be judged by the color of their skin, but by the content of their character.* His passion was that ALL prejudice would be eliminated from our culture, whether black or white.

I have a problem with some of these Martin Luther King wannabes. They have flamed a new kind of racial prejudice in our communities. The losers are the kids. They're always the ones in the cross hairs. They're always the target of every greedy, societal epidemic, harm, and danger. I have often said that when two elephants fight, only the grass suffers. The children are always the ones who lose.

Peter was preconditioned to keep his distance from the Gentiles. You don't eat the food that the Gentiles eat, and you don't go to their houses. His religious tradition was so strong that even when the Lord told him to eat, he could not do it. He was so bound up in religious tradition that when God said it was okay, he still said no. Isn't it crazy that some people are more loyal to their traditions than they are to the Lord?

I was raised with a group of people who were much more loyal to their tradition than they ever were to Jesus Christ. They spent more time fighting over what color to paint a wall than trying to figure out how to reach their city with the Gospel. Tradition can precondition us in a way where we can miss God, even when He is in our midst.

Peter was in conflict with God. In any conflict with God, you are going to lose. Peter did not know that there was a shift coming to the purposes of God. God had His eyes on the Gentiles. His heart was to include them in the Gospel story that was unfolding in the book of Acts.

> Our preconceived notions lock the door that God is trying to open in our lives.

God was moving Peter out of his comfort zone, taking him places where he never imagined he would go. Peter said, "I won't eat it." God said, "Yes, you will." Peter was being prepared to be one of the leaders in this new move of God. First, there had to be a major shift in Peter's way of thinking.

All of us have been preconditioned by our cultures, both geographical and religious. We all have a little bit of prejudice in us. These preconceived notions put a lock on the door that God is trying to open. Prejudicial attitudes keep people in bondage and prevent us from uniting together.

These attitudes must be exposed and expunged before God can use us. Before Peter can answer the knock at the door, he must finish his conversation with God. He must be convinced that what God calls clean is clean.

God showed him this truth in a vision. He saw something that challenged his preconceived ideas. The conversation with God gave him a peek into the heart of God and helped him understand that God's purposes were greater than he'd ever imagined.

Hungry people will see God, and that vision will open up new ways of thinking. You have to get to the place where you are no longer satisfied with the status quo. You want something different. You're tired of church as usual, and you want to experience more of God and become more involved in His purposes.

When you're hungry, hunger moves you. It moves you out of your tradition. It moves you out of your comfort zone. It moves you up to a different level. It moves you past the foolishness of things that have held you back. So, again I ask: How hungry are you?

Confronting our Comfort Zones

It is natural to want a life of ease and comfort. None of us want to see our lives disturbed by crisis or our traditions challenged by a dream. But God is not content to leave us in our comfort zones. He will confront us with the truth as He prepares us for the next step of the journey. God is pulling people out of cultures, away from their friends, away from their family, to a place where they would never choose on their own.

I like the way that American author, political activist, and lecturer Helen Keller (1880-1968) put it. Miss Keller was the first deaf and blind person to earn a Bachelor of Arts degree. She said, *"Character cannot be developed in ease and quiet. Only through experiences of trial and suffering can the soul be strengthened, vision cleared, ambition inspired and success achieved."*[57]

God will not leave you as you are. He will make you hungry. But you have to get to the place where you despise the place you are in. Get hungry!

I have watched staff members come and go here in New York. Those who are not hungry cannot live in this place. Their comfort zones will be confronted. Their attitudes will be exposed. Their traditional upbringing will be challenged. The hungry ones survive and grow and mature. The ones who are not hungry will return to their comfortable places.

God was taking Peter out of his comfort zone, preparing him for a new life apart from his religious traditions. No one likes the pain that comes with confrontation. This is the reason why people only have me come in once a year to speak in their churches. They could never take a full diet of Bill Wilson. I force people to look at themselves.

I am like the innocent child from the Danish fairy tale author Hans Christian Andersen (1805-1875), who loudly exclaimed, for the whole kingdom to hear, that the Emperor was not wearing any clothes, in his famous book *The Emperor's New Clothes*. The Emperor was as naked as the day he was born. He had no clothes to cover his nakedness! No one likes to be exposed for who they are. But there are times when it takes drastic measures to contest our place of security.

A good leader will confront the issues. He [or she] will reject the path of the enabler and become a partner in the process of healing. Problems left alone will not heal. It takes the work of the trained physician to identify the problem and to provide the cure. Ignoring the problem does not resolve the problem.

Going to the People

The final confrontation and preparation for Peter came with the knock at his door. Peter opened the door and was now staring at a bunch of Italian guys who had a request. "Come to our house and tell us what you have to say." Peter had been prepared for this moment. What did he do? He invited them in as his guests.

> We can no longer sit in our comfortable churches or behind our computers hoping people will come to us. We must go to where the hungry people are!

Peter went with them to the house of Cornelius. He arrived and preached the Gospel to them. Just as in Acts 2, the whole house of Cornelius was filled with the Holy Spirit, exactly what had happened in the Upper Room. They were hungry, and their hunger was filled on that day.

Peter was shocked at what happened. The Holy Spirit came to the Gentiles just as He had come to the Jews! A paradigm shift was put in motion. He was right in the middle of the sermon, and the

Gentiles were getting filled with the Holy Spirit! Revival hit the house of Cornelius. What was the paradigm shift? Instead of the people coming to us, *we will go to the people.*

We can no longer sit in our comfortable churches or behind our computers hoping people will come to us. We must take the initiative. We must go to where the hungry people are. We must become the initiators.

This work in New York would never have happened if I had waited for the children to come to me. At one point in my life I had to get up and go to where they were. It was not the most comfortable or safest place in the world. But it was where the kids were. Someone had to do it. I was hungry and became the volunteer.

The Church has to lead the way. But the problem is many people can't even get past their own issues. We cannot depend upon the government to resolve our issues. The Church was meant to lead the way.

Why was Peter at Simon the tanner's house? Why didn't he see that God was shifting His focus toward the Gentiles? Why didn't He understand that God loved the Gentiles as well? He was there because his religious traditions had not allowed him to see the opportunities that existed for him.

The journey had begun with his hunger. Even though he was blinded by tradition, he was hungry and his hunger made him a dreamer. Somewhere in his walk, somewhere in his ministry, he finally got it. I don't know where, but he got it. God was doing something in him. He was confronting him and preparing him. The cursing, the falling asleep in the Garden, the denying His Lord—it was all behind him.

He now saw something he had never seen before. He saw the Lord and the greatness of His plans and purposes. Hunger caused him to jump out of the boat and run to his Lord and now that same hunger had led him to the house of Cornelius.

Hunger will lead you past your insecurities and fears. Hunger will overcome all the supposed obstacles that stand in your way. Hunger will cause you to go to places you would never go to. Hunger will make you have dreams and visions. Those dreams will unlock doors.

It is my prayer for you that hunger will overtake your complacency and cause you to dream again. If you become hungry, then you will hear the knock at your door and a brand new world will open for you.

ENDNOTES

INTRODUCTION

1. http://thinkexist.com/quotation/it_is_not_the_critic_who_counts-not_the_man_who/12121.html

CHAPTER ONE

2. Don Williams Jr., http://thinkexist.com/quotation/the-road-of-life-twists-and-turns-and-no-two/763577.html

3. http://www.brainyquote.com/quotes/quotes/w/williamthr228289.html

4. http://www.quoteland.com/author.asp?AUTHOR_ID=2413

CHAPTER TWO

5. Charles Spurgeon, http://www.ministers-best-friend.com/Day-by-Day-the-Webs-LARGEST-Devotional-Opportunities-Fingertips-by-NewtonStein.html

6. http://www.hopeinthecities.org/node/27368

7. http://www.quotationspage.com/quote/1941.html

CHAPTER THREE

8. Joni Earecksen Tada, http://www.inspirational-quotations.com/faith-quotes.html

9. http://www.merriam-webster.com/dictionary/cliche

10. http://www.weddingvendors.com/music/lyrics/b/bill-withers/lean-on-me/

11. http://www.wisdomquotes.com/cat_compassion.html

12. http://thinkexist.com/quotation/let_us_touch_the_dying-the_poor-the_lonely_and/216343.html

13. http://www.brainyquote.com/quotes/keywords/tenacity.html

Chapter Four

14. Henri Nouwen, *Out of Solitude,* http://www.wisdomquotes.com/cat_friendship.html

15. Francis Schaeffer, *The Mark of a Christian,* IVP, Downer's Grove, Il., ©1976, *Pg. 8*

Chapter Five

16. Aesop's Fables, http://en.thinkexist.com/quotation/a_doubtful_friend_is_worse_than_a_certain_enemy/221811.html

17. Karmapa Urgyen Trinley Dorje, http://www.thedailymind.com/success/bad-company-are-your-friends-really-friends/

Chapter Six

18. William Arthur Ward, http://thinkexist.com/quotation/as_the_valley_gives_height_to_the_mountain-so_can/329860.html

19. http://thinkexist.com/quotation/creating_a_new_theory_is_not_like_destroying_an/326978.html

20. http://thinkexist.com/quotation/i_have_a_dream_that_one_day_every_valley_shall_be/215477.html

Chapter Seven

21. G.K. Chesterton, http://www.quotesdaddy.com/tag/Valley

22. http://net.bible.org/dictionary.php?word=Kidron%20Valley

23. *Best Thoughts: Selections from the Writings of Henry Drummond,*(Kessinger Publishing, Whitefish Montana 2005) Pg. 120

24. http://thinkexist.com/quotes/jim_elliot/

25. http://www.bibleplaces.com/elahvalley.htm

26. Malcolm, Gladwell, *The Tipping Point,*(Little, Brown and Company, Boston, 2000) Pg. 33

27. *The Tipping Point*, Pg. 92

28. *The Tipping Point, Pg.* 139

29. http://www.military-quotes.com/Sun-Tzu.htm

30. http://thinkexist.com/quotes/edward_de_bono/2.html

31. http://bibleatlas.org/valley_of_achor.htm

32. http://thinkexist.com/quotation/the_purpose_of_problems_is_to_push_you_toward/288418.html

Chapter Eight

33. Julius Caesar, http://www.brainyquote.com/quotes/quotes/j/juliuscaes399699.html

34. http://thinkexist.com/quotes/john_mcdonald/

35. http://www.quotegarden.com/patience.html

36. http://thinkexist.com/quotation/life_is_all_about_timing-the_unreachable_becomes/220324.html

Chapter Nine

37. Anais, Nin, http://thinkexist.com/quotation/life_is_a_process_of_becoming-a_combination_of/221101.html

38. http://www.wisdomquotes.com/003775.html

39. Marianne Williamson, http://thinkexist.com/quotes/marianne_williamson/2.html

Chapter Ten

40. Carlos Castaneda, http://thinkexist.com/quotes/carlos_castaneda/

41. http://thinkexist.com/quotes/harriet_beecher_stowe/

42. http://www.christiananswers.net/dictionary/sling.html

43. http://thinkexist.com/quotes/edgar_a._guest/

44. http://thinkexist.com/quotation/a_leader-once_convinced_a_particular_course_of/337325.html

CHAPTER ELEVEN

45. William Blake, http://quotationsbook.com/quote/15347/

46. Andrew Bonar, *The Christian Treasury,* Religious Tract and Book Society of Scotland. Edinburgh, © 1858, Pg. 160

47. http://en.wikipedia.org/wiki/Hebron

48. International Standard Bible Encyclopedia, http://bibleencyclopedia.com/kedesh.htm

49. http://www.ancientsandals.com/overviews/shechem.htm

CHAPTER TWELVE

50. http://thinkexist.com/quotation/one_of_the_annoying_things_about_believing_in/323848.html

51. http://homepage.mac.com/shanerosenthal/reformationink/bbwprodigal.htm

52. http://www.goodreads.com/author/quotes/66573.Brother_Lawrence

53. *The Return of the Prodigal Son,* Henri Nouwen, Doubleday, New York, © 1992, Pg. 6

54. http://www.illspot.net/forum/topics/1271544:Topic:70323

CHAPTER THIRTEEN

55. http://thinkexist.com/quotation/passion-it-lies-in-all-of-us-sleeping-waiting/411216.html

56. http://www.brainyquote.com/quotes/authors/r/roger_bannister_2.html

57. http://thinkexist.com/quotation/character_cannot_be_developed_in_ease_and_quiet/13579.html

ABOUT THE AUTHOR

BILL WILSON IS THE Founder and Senior Pastor of "Metro Ministries," the world's largest Sunday School, and an international Christian humanitarian organization with headquarters in Brooklyn, NY. "Metro" reaches more than 40,000 inner-city children and their families every week in New York City and around the world. Based on his principle that "it is easier to build boys and girls than to repair men and women," this successful, relationship-centered pattern is currently recognized as one of the top ten influential ministries having the greatest impact around the world today.

Abandoned at 12 years old by his alcoholic mother, Bill's body still bears the scars of several childhood disorders. The painful beginning to his story is the same one he hears from the children he now reaches out to—that they have been abandoned by their families, society and even the agencies who are supposed to care for them. From a timid young boy, he has grown into a messenger of hope in the extreme darkness of today's inner city...and the price for his commitment has been high.

"Pastor Bill," as he is known to the kids, has been hospitalized repeatedly and continues to be treated for a gunshot wound to his mouth and jaw following a robbery. Personal adversity has only strengthened his resolve to do "whatever it takes." Bill Wilson has always believed that what happens *in* you is more important than what happens *to* you.

In 2007, renovations began on the "Metro World Ministries Center." Upon completion, this building will provide facilities to add programs that include obtaining a GED, parenting classes, and food services, as well as Bill Wilson's extensive training program that has proved successful in duplicating his commitment to reach millions of children with the love of Christ.

Pastor Bill speaks at leadership conferences and pastor's schools around the world focusing on reaching families, children, and the cities they live in. His book, ***Whose Child Is This?*** has been translated in 25 languages and his weekly television program, "In the Crosshairs," began airing in 2005. Check local listings for broadcast times in your area. The curriculum developed through this ministry is tested and proven in the hardcore, inner-city culture of New York before being translated into four languages and utilized in hundreds of cities worldwide using Bill Wilson's unique concept of "Sidewalk Sunday School."